Buses, Trams and Trolleybuses of Scotland and Ireland 1950s-1970s

Buses, Trams and Trolleybuses of Scotland and Ireland 1950s-1970s

The operators and their vehicles

Part 2: Glasgow and Ireland
Henry Conn

SLP
Silver Link Publishing Ltd

© Henry Conn 2012

All rights reserved. No part of this publication may be reproduced, stored in a retrieval system or transmitted, in any form or by any means, electronic, mechanical, photocopying, recording or otherwise, without prior permission in writing from Silver Link Publishing Ltd.

First published in 2012

British Library Cataloguing in Publication Data

A catalogue record for this book is available from the British Library.

ISBN 978 1 85794 401 3

Title page: No E121 (AZD 184) was a CIE-bodied Leyland L2 new to CIE in April 1964. It is seen here some years later passing along the shore of Lough Finn working the 16.45 departure from Ballybofey westwards to Glenties, which is 'Gleannta' in Gaelic, as shown on the destination blind.

Silver Link Publishing Ltd
The Trundle
Ringstead Road
Great Addington
Kettering
Northants NN14 4BW

Tel/Fax: 01536 330588
email: sales@nostalgiacollection.com
Website: www.nostalgiacollection.com

Printed and bound in the Czech Republic

All photographs not otherwise credited were taken by the author or are from his collection. Those labelled 'transporttreasury.co.uk' are obtainable from Transport Treasury.

Acknowledgements

Many of the photographs within this book have come from my collection, but my most sincere thanks go to David Clarke for allowing continuing and much-appreciated access to his wonderful collection of negatives and slides. David's portraits from the early 1950s through to the early 1960s of the trams of Glasgow are rare and exceptional. Many thanks also to Geoff Gould and Phil Sposito, and to Transport Treasury for safely archiving many of my negatives and slides.

The PSV publications of all the operators illustrated, and many early issues of *Buses Illustrated*, were vital sources of information.

Contents

Introduction	6
Glasgow Corporation	8
Belfast Corporation	96
Coras Iompair Eireann	102
Lough Swilly	120
Northern Ireland Road Transport Board/Ulster Transport Authority/Ulsterbus	123

If only the roads of today were as quiet as this! This is standard Glasgow hex-dash tram No 76 at Tollcross terminus on 4 June 1959. *David Clarke*

Introduction

At the busy Bridgeton Cross junction in Glasgow on 4 June 1959 is 'Cunarder' tram No 1343. The shelter was built in 1875 and became affectionately known as the 'Bridgeton Cross Umbrella'. It and the clock were made in Port Dundas by George Smith & Co at their Sun foundry. The tower in front of the 'Umbrella' is a signal cabin, which was used to control the comings and goings of trams at the five-way junction here. *David Clarke*

This is the second volume of three that will cover operators in Scotland and Ireland. This volume is dedicated to the buses, trams and trolleybuses of Glasgow Corporation and the buses and trolleybuses of Northern Ireland and the Republic of Ireland.

The Glasgow tram system not only operated in the city but also reached the encircling towns of Clydebank, Milngavie, Airdrie, Rutherglen, Barrhead, Paisley and Renfrew, and all are featured in this volume. By 1949 the tramway route mileage was at its maximum of 134, and in 1952 there were 1,150 cars operating 32 routes from 11 depots. During 1924 the first bus route was operated, and by 1933 there were 332 buses operating 15 services with a route mileage of 155. The trolleybuses began as an experiment on 3 April 1949, and their success led to a small group of trolleybus services being built up until 1958; there were six routes operated by a total of 178 trolleybuses.

In October 1955 Glasgow Corporation decided to abandon its tram routes outside the city boundary, and the

INTRODUCTION

routes to Paisley, Renfrew, Barrhead, Cambuslang, Airdrie and Milngavie had all been withdrawn by May 1957. Over the next few years the trams gave way to buses, and on 4 September 1962 the trams ceased to operate in Glasgow. By July 1963 Glasgow Corporation's revenue-earning fleet was made up of 1,334 buses, of which 101 were Leyland PDR1/1s, and 178 trolleybuses.

The Belfast trolleybus system was the only one in Ireland, and opened on 28 March 1938 to gradually replace the city's trams. It was the second largest fleet in the UK after London, and at its peak had 17 routes operated by a maximum fleet of 245 trolleybuses. It ceased operations on 12 May 1968.

Bus operations in Belfast had begun in 1926, and by April 1973, when Citybus took over the Corporation's fleet, there were 350 buses.

On 1 October 1935 the Northern Ireland Road Transport Board came into being, and absorbed 434 buses from the Belfast & County Down Railway, the Great Northern Railway, the Northern Counties Committee, the Belfast Omnibus Company and H. M. S. Catherwood Ltd. The Great Northern Railway only gave up the routes north of the border at this time, the remainder being taken over by Coras Iompair Eireann 23 years later. By the end of the 1930s the NIRTB had taken over most of the operators in the province, then in 1948 the NIRTB buses and the entire rail network merged to form the Ulster Transport Authority. The trams, trolleybuses and buses of Belfast Corporation were not affected by this merger.

UTA became Ulsterbus Ltd in April 1967 and the new company acquired a very mixed and ageing fleet of AEC Reliances, Leyland Titans, Leyland Tigers, Leopards, Royal Tigers, Olympics and Tiger Cubs, Albion Aberdonians, Bedford SB5s, VAS1s, a VAL 14 and a few Austin 20-seaters. Ulsterbus began to purchase single-deckers, and in 1968 20 Bristol RELLs were placed in service in Derry; eventually a total of 620 RELLs were to be operated by Ulsterbus.

Lough Swilly first began operating buses in 1929, and until 1960 most of the vehicles were purchased new, which included the first-ever Leyland Atlantean in Ireland. From 1962, however, bus purchases were sourced from UK operators and this continued until the next new buses, Bristol LHs, were purchased in 1971. Leyland Leopards were purchased in 1968 and between that year and 2001 a total of 266 were operated by the company.

Coras Iompair Eireann was the result of the amalgamation in January 1945 of two bus fleets, Dublin United Transport and the Great Southern Railways. A total of 688 buses were taken over by CIE, and also included was the Dublin tram system. A fleet of all-Leyland Titans arrived in 1948 and 1949, and with these in service the last Dublin tram operated in July 1949. By the mid-1950s CIE had largely replaced all of its pre-war single-deck buses and coaches with newer, larger vehicles, as well as increasing its numbers of double-deckers. Production of CIE buses from 1956 to 1961 was exclusively double-deckers, and 377 Leyland Titans and three AEC Regents entered service during that period. The year 1961 also saw the introduction of CIE's first Leyland Leopards, the E class, as well as its last new AECs; these were three Regent Vs, which replaced trains on the Waterford to Tramore branch line. The Leyland Leopard L2 began to enter service from August 1961 onwards and a further 144 were bodied at Spa Road works in 1962, 1963 and 1964. Entry into service of the final pair took place in January 1965. The first CIE Leyland Atlantean entered service in Dublin on route 19 on 29 November 1966.

Enjoy the nostalgia!

Glasgow Corporation

Horse-car operation by the Glasgow Tramways & Omnibus Company began on 19 August 1872, on a line leased to the company by Glasgow Corporation. In 1891 negotiations for the purchase of the premises, plant and equipment from Glasgow Tramways failed, but Glasgow Corporation began to purchase premises and equipment to operate the 31 miles of tram track, and by 30 June 1894, when the Corporation took over the system, nine depots had been built and 290 trams and 3,500 horses had been purchased. Pinkston power station was built and began to supply power on 24 April 1901. By 1902 265 horse-cars had been withdrawn and the remainder converted to electric traction.

In 1922 Airdrie & Coatbridge Tramways was acquired, and a year later the Paisley & District Tramways Company was taken over. On 8 December 1924 the first bus service commenced, between Greendyke Street and Shakespeare Street. The Standard tram was the backbone of the tram fleet; 693 cars with round dash panels were built between 1898 and 1910, and 312 with hexagonal dash panels between 1901 and 1924. The type assumed its final form when the cars were reconditioned between 1928 and 1930.

The first double-decker buses, Leyland TD1s, arrived in 1928, and by 1933 there were 324 double- and single-deck buses running eight feeder services for the trams. The first oil-engined buses, 20 Albion Venturers with Gardner engines, arrived in 1935. No new tramcars had been built since 1928, due to the success of the reconditioning of the Standard cars. During 1937 a new car, built for the Empire Exhibition at Bellahouston, entered service, and was named 'Coronation'. During the war Glasgow received 90 buses; just after the war the Corporation applied for powers to build bus and trolleybus bodies, and this was granted. The first post-war car was No 1005, and between 1948 and 1952 100 'Cunarder' cars were built, incorporating the best features of the 'Coronations'.

On 3 April 1949 trolleybus services began, and a small group of services were built up from then until 1958. By 1950 80% of the trams were more than 35 years old, but Glasgow continued to be faithful to the tramway system and purchased 46 'Green Goddess' trams from Liverpool between 1953 and 1955. Six new tramcars, Nos 1393 to 1398, were completed in 1954, the last cars to be built for the fleet; they were of the 'Coronation' style but had bogies and motors from Liverpool tramcars that had been damaged in a depot fire.

Opposite: On 19 April 1953 service 1 was extended from Dennistoun to Springfield Road or Dalmornock, and Dalmornock depot commenced operation of the service. Just over three years later the Dalmuir service was curtailed at certain times to Scotstoun West, and on 7 May 1956 services were extended from Scotstoun West to Yoker on Mondays to Fridays between 12 noon and 2.00pm. This is Standard hex-dash No 13 heading for Scotstoun West on Great Western Road at Woodlands Drive on 6 June 1959. The car behind No 13 is a Sunbeam Mark III, which was built between 1954 and 1957 and in 1955 could be yours for £1,191. *David Clarke*

However, by May 1957 the tram routes to Paisley, Renfrew, Barrhead, Cambuslang, Airdrie and Milngavie had been withdrawn. In November of that year the Corporation's first 30-foot bus, FYS 999, an Alexander-bodied Daimler CVD650-30, appeared at the Scottish Motor Show, entering service in 1958. This was followed by the first Leyland Atlantean, FYS 998, but subsequent deliveries were Leyland PD3/2s and AEC Regent Vs.

Tram routes continued to be withdrawn, and on 4 September 1962 tram operations ceased. The fleet strength in 1963 was 1,334 buses and 178 trolleybuses, and the Leyland PDR1/1 would be the standard bus for the Corporation for a number of years to come.

Route 1

Right: **This is Standard hex-dash No 180 heading for Dalmuir at Whitecrook Street on Glasgow Road, Clydebank, on 11 June 1959, near the main gate of John Brown's shipyard. Started by J. & G. Thomson in 1871, the yard built up steadily, and by 1880 employed 2,000. In 1899, however, it ran into financial difficulties and was taken over by the Sheffield steelmaker John Brown & Company. It then prospered, and in 1907 it launched the** *Lusitania*, **which at that time was the largest ship ever built. As well as building ocean-going liners it also built warships, including HMS** *Hood*, **which was launched in 1918. The prosperity lasted 20 years, but following the Great War the yard went into decline. The gloom was lifted with the order for the** *Queen Mary*, **launched in September 1934, and the** *Queen Elizabeth*, **which followed in September 1938. The last great ship under the John Brown name was the** *QE2*, **launched in September 1967. In 1968 the company became part of Upper Clyde Shipbuilders, and was bought by Marathon, an American oil-rig firm, in 1972, and by UIE in 1980, but went into decline and closed for the last time in 2002, by this time part of the Kvaerner Group. The yard is now demolished.** David Clarke

Below: **This is Standard hex-dash No 286 on Great Western Road on 8 June 1959, near the boating pond known as Bingham's Pond, created in the 1880s on the site of old brick and coal pits. The boathouse was built around 1885 and became a tea room. The eastern part of the site was sold in 1956 and in the 1960s that part of the pond was infilled and a hotel and car park built. The remaining part of the site was acquired by the Corporation as a public park.** David Clarke

GLASGOW CORPORATION ROUTE 3

Tram 401 is a Standard round-dash car with a flat lower-deck roof, and this view was taken on New City Road at St Peter Street on 26 June 1959. Less than a year later, on 12 March 1960, route 1 was replaced by bus service 58. The bus behind No 401 is an all-Leyland PD1. *David Clarke*

Route 3

In May 1938 route 3 ran between the University and Mosspark, and the trams to operate it came from Maryhill and Newlands depots. During August 1945 the portion of the service operated by Maryhill was transferred to Newlands. This is Standard round-dash car No 360 on Eglinton Street on 22 August 1958; on 4 January of the following year the University-bound cars were diverted to run to Park Road. *David Clarke*

Above: **On Mosspark Boulevard at the junction of Arran Drive on 26 August 1958 is 'Cunarder' No 1326, which entered service in 1950. Following the experimental No 1005, between 1948 and 1952 100 'Cunarders' were built by Glasgow Corporation at its Coplawhill works. In the background is Bellahouston Park, which** until the late 19th century was rural farmland and part of the Maxwell estate. The land was purchased by Glasgow Corporation in 1895 and opened as a public park in 1896, with adjacent land added between 1901 and 1903. *David Clarke*

Left: **This is Torridon Avenue in Dumbreck on 26 August 1959, and approaching the camera working route 3 is No 1215, a 'Coronation' car built in 1938 with EMB lightweight bogies and four BTH 109 35hp motors. This view was taken at 12.54pm, and we can assume that the gentleman by the van on the left with his arms folded is having his lunch break.** *David Clarke*

Above: In January 1959, to allow repairs to the bridge in Gibson Street, the University terminus was closed and the trams were diverted to Park Road; they subsequently did not return to the University terminus. This is 'Cunarder' No 1258 at the Park Road terminus on 5 June 1959. *David Clarke*

Below: 'Cunarder' No 1211 is on Albert Drive passing Coplawhill works on 14 September 1959. In addition to being one of the nine depots built in readiness for the Glasgow Corporation operation of the tramcar network, Coplawhill was also established as the repair and overhaul facility. With electrification and the opening of further depots, it was extended and turned over solely to manufacturing and overhauling the tramcar fleet, and, in its final years, the scrapping of some trams and assembly of bus bodywork. The depot closed in 1962. *David Clarke*

14 BUSES, TRAMS AND TROLLEYBUSES OF SCOTLAND & IRELAND

Above: **Standard hex-dash tram No 234 is seen in Woodlands Road on 10 September 1959. In the background is St Jude's Church, which was designed by John Burnet and completed in 1875; it is now protected as a category B listed building.** *David Clarke*

Route 4

Below: **Route 4 in May 1938 ran between Keppochhill Road and Renfrew Airport; in 1940 the latter terminus was renamed Renfrew South. On 1 April 1951 the route was extended from Keppochhill to Springburn, and in early February 1954 from Renfrew South to Paisley North. Standing at Paisley North terminus on 7 July 1956 is Standard round-dash No 512. The Renfrew and Paisley services were abandoned on 11 May of the following year.** *David Clarke*

Above: **This is Standard hex-dash No 78 at Harland & Wolff on Govan Road, also on 7 July 1956.** In 1912 Harland & Wolff acquired the Govan 'New Yard' and the Middleton Yard from London & Glasgow Shipbuilding & Engineering Co, together with the Govan 'Old Yard' from Mackie & Thomson; the three yards were amalgamated and redeveloped to provide a total of seven building berths, a fitting-out basin and extensive workshops. Harland & Wolff specialised in building tankers and cargo ships at Govan. The yard closed in 1962, when the company opted to consolidate its operations in Belfast. *David Clarke*

Below: **This is 'Cunarder' No 1339 on Paisley Road at Morrison Street on 24 June 1958.** The car passing in the opposite direction is a Vauxhall Velox EIPV, which was produced between 1951 and 1957. In 1952 you could buy this car for £833, and just over 235,000 were made at the Luton factory. The bus in the background is an Alexander-bodied Leyland PD2. *David Clarke*

Just 7 minutes later the camera captured Standard hex-dash No 54. Just behind the tram is a Western SMT Guy Arab, and in the distance is a Western SMT ECW-bodied Bristol LD. *David Clarke*

Above: **Standard hex-dash No 101 is seen in Renfrew High Street on 13 July 1956.** In the background is Renfrew Town Hall; its design is a mix of French and Gothic styles, featuring a square tower 105 feet high with corbelled turrets at each corner. The architect was James Lamb of Paisley. The Memorial Stone was laid in 1872 with a street procession and grand ceremony and the building was completed and opened in October 1873. It was a replacement for the old tollbooth, which had served as both town hall and jail for 200 years.
David Clarke

Right: **Another Standard hex-dash tram, No 152, is seen on Springburn Road at Blenheim Street on 24 June 1958.** The van on the left is an LD. These were sold under both the Morris and Austin banner, and were produced in Birmingham at Adderley Park, which had been part of the Morris empire. The Austin was badged as the 1-ton (LD1) and the 1.5-ton (LD2), launched in December 1954. Initially it was only available with a petrol engine of 2.2 litres, but at the beginning of 1955 both were available with a 2.2-litre diesel engine as an option. The LD2's larger capacity was achieved by a raised roof and a longer body. It also had a stiffer suspension all round, and a lower rear axle ratio. The price in January 1956 ex-works in grey primer for a 1.5-ton diesel was £877, but by June 1959 it had gone down to £833 due to purchase tax being removed from commercial vehicles in that year's budget.
David Clarke

Above: **This is Standard hex-dash No 9 on St Georges Road at Garscube Road on 26 June 1958. The depots providing trams for route 4 were Possilpark and Govan, and the last tram ran on 6 September 1958, to be replaced by bus route 53.** *David Clarke*

Below: **On the same day Standard hex-dash No 124 was photographed on Keppochhill Road at Coldstream Place.** *David Clarke*

GLASGOW CORPORATION ROUTE 5

Route 5 and 5A

Above: **On 10 June 1945 route 5 became Clarkston to Kelvinside, and a few months later, on 9 September, the terminus was moved south along Hyndland Road to Hyndland Station. This is Standard hex-dash No 110 on Hyndland Road on 4 July 1956.** *David Clarke*

On Byres Road at the junction of Roxburgh Street on the same day is 'Coronation' No 1239. Following closely behind are an AEC Regent V and an AEC Regent III. *David Clarke*

Above: **On Battlefield Road there was a short section of reserved track laid in sett paving rather than ballast, and Standard round-dash No 888 is photographed there on 5 July 1956. The lone car on the right is a Morris Minor Series II with the split windscreen; this model was produced between 1952 and 1956, and in 1952 could be bought new for £631.** *David Clarke*

Below: **On 5 July 1953 the service to Clarkston was withdrawn and the route became Holmlea Road to Kelvinside. This is Standard round-dash No 472 with 'Coronation' No 1179 behind at Holmlea Road, Cathcart terminus, also on 5 July 1956.** *David Clarke*

GLASGOW CORPORATION ROUTE 5 and 5A

'Coronation' No 1241 passes Queen's Park Station on 5 July 1956. The station was opened on 1 March 1886 and still retains its original island platform and station building; the line was electrified in May 1962. *David*

Clarke
Standard round-dash No 420 is seen at the junction of Renfield Street and Argyle Street on 6 July 1956. The car is an Austin A40 Somerset, which was introduced in 1952 and was basically a rebodied A40 Devon using the same basic mechanical components. Its appearance carried over the rather bulbous but smaller version of the A70 Hereford. Although it had a slightly more powerful engine than the Devon, it was still underpowered if fully loaded. For £7 you could have a sliding roof as a factory option. The two millionth car produced at the Longbridge plant was an A40 Somerset. In 1954 the range was dropped, to be replaced by the all-new square look of the A40/50 Cambridge. *David Clarke*

Route 6

Above: **In 1938 route 6 trams travelled between Riddrie and Dalmuir West. In November 1951, however, the service to Dalmuir West was stopped at weekends and was later discontinued apart from the odd special. This is 'Coronation' No 1168 on Sauchiehall Street at Dalhouse Street on 24 June 1958. The large car on the right is a Jaguar Mark VII, identifiable by the two-piece front windscreen. This car was produced between 1951 and 1956 and during that time just under 31,000 were produced. The Mark VII had a top speed of 101mph and in 1952 cost £1,693 new.** *David Clarke*

Below: **Standing at the terminus of route 6 in Aitken Street on 25 June 1956 is 'Coronation' No 1216. The car on the left is an Austin A40 Somerset and the estate car on the right is a Standard 10.** *David Clarke*

GLASGOW CORPORATION ROUTE 6

Top: **These three photographs were taken on 10 June 1959. In the first, approaching the camera is Standard round-dash No 288. The nearest advertising board is for Chivers jelly. Chivers first began making jam in 1873; in 1889, to ensure a permanent, not seasonal, experienced workforce, the company diversified into marmalade, closely followed by the first clear, commercial dessert jelly.** *David Clarke*

Centre: **Heading for Scotstoun on Sauchiehall Street at Royal Crescent is Standard hex-dash No 76.** *David Clarke*

Bottom: **This is Dumbarton Road at the junction of Victoria Park Street, and nearest the camera is Standard round-dash No 311. Following is Standard hex-dash No 145. On 1 November 1959 the Riddrie to Scotstoun tram route was replaced by bus route 59.** *David Clarke*

Route 7

Above: **The 7 route in January 1938 ran between Millerston or Riddrie to Criagton Road and was numbered 31/31a going east and 32/32a going west. On 6 February 1938 the route was extended to Bellahouston, Jura Street south end. As part of the renumbering of the tram system that took place on 3 May 1938, the route became No 7. At Riddrie terminus on 5 July 1956 is Standard hex-dash car No 153.** *David Clarke*

Below: **Crossing the busy junction of Cumbernauld Road and Edinburgh Road on the same day is another hex dash Standard, No 272.** *David Clarke*

GLASGOW CORPORATION ROUTE 7

Above: **This is the very busy Duke Street on 6 July 1956, and approaching the camera en route to Riddrie is Standard hex-dash No 67.** *David Clarke*

Below: **This wonderful photograph of Standard round-dash No 739 and Standard hex-dash No 158 was taken on Ballater Street on the same day.** *David Clarke*

Above: **The reconstruction of the buildings at Gorbals Cross began in 1872 to plans drawn up by John Carrick, the City Architect. Following the contemporary Parisian fashion, the buildings were set at angles to create an open diamond-shaped plaza. In 1878 a drinking fountain and large clock tower was built here by George Smith & Co, but was sadly later demolished, to be replaced by the clock seen in this view. The two trams are Standard hex-dash Nos 1039 and 266, seen again on 6 July 1956.** *David Clarke*

Below: **Standard round-dash No 344 is seen on Govan Road, with Prince's Docks in the background, on 7 July 1956. Prince's Dock was originally known as Cessnock Dock and was built for the Clyde Navigation Trust between 1893 and 1897. The formal opening was performed by the Duchess of York on 10 September 1895, and it was reputed to have cost £1,250,000 to build. The ships of the Canadian Pacific Company, the Anchor-Donaldson Line and many others berthed at Prince's Dock.** *David Clarke*

Route 8

Above: **On 15 August 1943 the 1938 services 8 and 8A were reorganised and renumbered 8 and 25. Route 8 became Millerston or Riddrie to Newlands, Merrylee, Giffnock or Rouken Glen. This is Giffnock on 24 June 1958, and working route 8 is 'Cunarder' No 1315, new in 1949.** *David Clarke*

Below: **At the junction of Pollokshaws Road and Maxwell Street on 23 June 1958 is Standard round-dash No 413. Note the elevated advert for Haig. The Haig whisky distilling dynasty can rightfully lay claim to be the oldest Scotch whisky distillers, having being active for more than 300 years, the first record of Haig distilling dating from 1655. The lorry behind No 413 is a Leyland Comet and the van is a Ford 100E.** *David Clarke*

Above: **This is Standard hex-dash No 103 on Fenwick Road at Otterburn Drive, also on 23 June 1958.** *David Clarke*

Below: **Passing Alexandra Park en route to Millerston on 25 June 1958 is Standard hex-dash car No 99. The City Improvement Trustees of Glasgow purchased land from Mr Walter Stewart in 1866 and over the next few years, using unemployed labourers, the renovation of the land was undertaken. The park was officially opened and named after Princess Alexandra of Denmark in 1870.** *David Clarke*

GLASGOW CORPORATION ROUTE 9

Route 9

Above: On 3 May 1938 the route between Dalmuir West and London Road or Auchenshuggle was renumbered 9. This is 'Cunarder' No 1340 at Auchenshuggle on 4 June 1959. *David Clarke*

Below: Because of the tendency of the Kilmarnock Bogie trams to derail on curves they were allocated to routes that had few of them. Route 9 had very few curves in its entire length of nearly 12 miles. This is Kilmarnock Bogie No 1102 on Argyle Street near Hope Street on 8 June 1959. It was built by Hurst Nelson of Motherwell and had Kilmarnock Engineering maximum traction bogies and two 60hp motors. *David Clarke*

Above: **Nearest the camera in this view taken at Auchenshuggle on 8 June 1959 is Standard round-dash No 825. No 1137 in the background is a Kilmarnock Bogie tram, built by Brush of Loughborough.** *David Clarke*

Below: **On 10 June 1959 'Cunarder' No 1309 crosses Partick Bridge, which was built in 1878. In the background is the Kelvin Hall, which dates from 1927 and was designed to house large-scale exhibitions.** *David Clarke*

Above: The new Dalmuir swing bridge on the Forth & Clyde Canal was opened on 10 February 1915, and crossing it on 11 June 1959 is Brush-built Kilmarnock Bogie tram No 1133. On 7 September 1959 the swing bridge was closed for repairs, and all trams turned at Dalmuir; the service to Dalmuir West was resumed on 1 August 1960. *David Clarke*

Below: At Dalmuir West on 12 May 1962 is 'Cunarder' No 1341. Just a few weeks later the tram service to Dalmuir West was curtailed at Yoker, and the last trams in Glasgow ran to Auchenshuggle on 4 September of that year. *David Clarke*

Route 10

Above: On 19 April 1953 the Kelvinside and Circle Parkhead tram route 10 was withdrawn and the service became Kelvinside and London Road. Standard trams were operated on this route until 1955, when 'Coronations' and 'Cunarders' gradually took over. This is Standard round-dash No 296 in the summer of 1954. *transporttreasury.co.uk*

Below: What a great way to read your newspaper! This is Standard hex-dash No 681 in the summer of 1954. On 4 June 1960 route 10 was withdrawn without replacement by a bus service. *transporttreasury.co.uk*

GLASGOW CORPORATION ROUTE 12

Route 12

Above: Route 12, Mount Florida and Paisley Road Toll, was operated by Standards only, due to the route having tight curves. At Mount Florida terminus on 5 July 1956 is Standard hex-dash No 100. The van is a Ford E83W 10cwt, which was aimed at the small haulage, trade and merchant market; it was powered by the 1,172cc Ford 10hp side-valve engine with a three-speed gearbox, and was heavily geared down in the rear axle. The E83W was a simple, slow but sturdy and lovable little commercial, which continued to serve well into the 1960s in good numbers. *David Clarke*

Below: At Paisley Road Toll on 7 July 1956 is Standard round-dash No 986. Trolleybus route 108 commenced on 15 November 1958 between Mount Florida and Paisley Road Toll; this was the last tram route to be converted to trolleybuses, operated by a fleet of 35-foot-long single-deck trolleybuses. *David Clarke*

34 BUSES, TRAMS AND TROLLEYBUSES OF SCOTLAND & IRELAND

GLASGOW CORPORATION ROUTE 12

Main picture: **Working route 12 on Seaward Street, also on 7 July 1956, is Standard hex-dash No 23.** *David Clarke*

Opposite top: **The three different railway stations at Shields Junction in the Pollokshields area of Glasgow – Pollokshields, Shields Road and Shields – which had existed side-by-side since the mid-1880s, were combined to form a new Shields Road station on 1 April 1925. The station closed on 14 February 1966. Passing the station on 7 July 1956 is Standard round-dash car No 727.** *David Clarke*

Above: **Strathbungo railway station was originally part of the Glasgow, Barrhead & Kilmarnock Joint Railway and was opened on 1 December 1877; it closed to passengers on 28 May 1962. Passing the station on 6 July 1956 is Standard hex-dash No 23.** *David Clarke*

36   BUSES, TRAMS AND TROLLEYBUSES OF SCOTLAND & IRELAND

At the junction of Alison Street and Pollokshaws Road on 7 July 1956 is Standard round-dash No 727. *David Clarke*

Route 14

On 4 October 1953 route 14 was extended to Arden, and seen there on 6 July 1956 is Standard round-dash No 713. *David Clarke*

GLASGOW CORPORATION ROUTE 14

Above: **Standard hex-dash No 209 runs along the reserved/private track at Nitshill Road on the same day.** *David Clarke*

Left: **On 3 April 1949 service 14 was extended from Spiersbridge to Cross Stobs (Caplethill Road south end). At the terminus on 6 July 1956 is Standard round-dash No 928.** *David Clarke*

38   BUSES, TRAMS AND TROLLEYBUSES OF SCOTLAND & IRELAND

Above: **At the junction of Spiersbridge Road and Rouken Glen Road on 24 June 1958 is 'Coronation' No 1169.** *David Clarke*

Opposite top: **This excellent view of Standard round-dash No 576 at the junction of Thornliebank Road and Boydstone Road was also taken on 24 June 1958. Thornliebank railway station, beneath the bridge on the right, was opened by Busby Railway on 1 October 1881.** *David Clarke*

Main picture: **En route to Arden on Sauchiehall Street at the junction of Royal Crescent on 2 September 1959 is Standard hex-dash No 209. Two months later route 14 was withdrawn and replaced by bus route 57. The car parked to the right of the tram is a Fiat 1100/103, which was produced between 1953 and 1962. In the background is a British Road Services Leyland eight-wheel rigid lorry.** *David Clarke*

GLASGOW CORPORATION ROUTE 14

Standard round-dash No 363 is seen at Arden on 9 September 1959. The bus is ex-Southdown No 102 (BUF 202), which I think is a Leyland TD3 that was new in the mid-1930s. A number of Southdown's Leyland TDs that were new between 1934 and 1939 were rebodied by a selection of bodybuilders between 1946 and 1950. *David Clarke*

Route 15

On 15 August 1943 route 15 became Anderston Cross and Baillieston or Airdrie, and the depots providing trams for this route were Parkhead and Coatbridge. At Baillieston on 13 July 1956 is 'Coronation' No 1180. *David Clarke*

Just over half an hour after the previous picture, this view of 'Coronation' No 1247 was taken in Argyle Street. The car heading away from the camera is a Vauxhall Cresta E with, I think, an Inverness registration (JST). The van parked to the right is a Ford and the larger van to the left is an Austin K8. The K8 was produced from 1947 until 1954 and could be purchased in grey primer in March 1947 for £535. By May 1953 the cost was £841, and by the end of production in September 1954 around 26,500 had been built. *David Clarke*

Above and below: **Two 'Coronations' feature in these 22 August 1959 views, No 1226 at the junction of Baillieston Road and Blackcroft Road, and No 1263 at Garrowhill.** *Both David Clarke*

GLASGOW CORPORATION ROUTE 3

Above: **Between 1953 and 1955 Glasgow Corporation acquired 47 'Green Goddess' trams from Liverpool Corporation, and the first to be put into service was No 1006 in October 1953. This is No 1056, numerically the last of the batch, at Baillieston on 22 September 1959.** *David Clarke*

Below: **The 'Coronation' trams were first introduced in December 1936, and by the end of 1937 eight had been built. At Airdrie terminus on 4 July 1956 are Nos 1145 and 1147, both new in 1937.** *David Clarke*

This is 'Coronation' No 1163 at Coatdyke on, 4 July 1956 and the bus behind is a Scottish Omnibuses AEC Regent III. The car on the left is a Hillman Husky, which was produced between 1954 and 1957. Just over 42,000 of this three-door estate were sold, and in 1954 you could purchase one for £564. *David Clarke*

Above: **This is Stirling Street in Airdrie on the same day, and approaching the camera is 'Coronation' No 1153. The bus in the background is a Scottish Omnibuses AEC Regent III.** *David Clarke*

Top: **This is tram No 1247 passing Albion Rovers FC ground at Cliftonhill, also on 4 July 1956. Albion Rovers was formed in 1882, but the club did not move to Cliftonhill until 1919.** *David Clarke*

Centre: **Standing outside Coatbridge depot on 4 July 1956 is 'Coronation' No 1172. The depot, formerly belonging to Airdrie & Coatbridge Tramways, was acquired by Glasgow Corporation in 1921. It had opened in 1904 and closed in November 1956 when the tram service to Airdrie was withdrawn.** *David Clarke*

Bottom: **'Coronation' No 1172 is seen in Coatbridge High Street at the Fountain on the same day. The Whitelaw Fountain in the background is a drinking fountain with finely carved stone detailing designed by Hugh Haugh MacLure, who was an architect and civil engineer working from Sauchiehall Street in Glasgow and who predominantly worked on railways and road bridges. The fountain is dedicated to Alexander Whitelaw, industrialist and partner in the local firm of Gartsherrie Iron, who in 1872 organised the relocation of the railway line away from the main street to create a civic space.** *David Clarke*

GLASGOW CORPORATION ROUTE 15

Top: 'Coronation' No 1233 passes Coatbridge Central station on 3 July 1956. The station was originally named simply Coatbridge, but gained the suffix 'Central' in 1953 after the 1826 Monkland & Kirkintilloch Railway station named Coatbridge Central closed in 1951. The existing station is the result of a rebuild by the Caledonian Railway in 1900. *David Clarke*

Centre: This is 'Green Goddess' No 1052 on Baillieston Road on 9 June 1959. This tram had an EMB lightweight bogie and four GEC WT184a 35hp motors. *David Clarke*

Bottom: Working route 15 in August 1960 is 'Coronation' No 1247. Travelling in the opposite direction en route to Edinburgh through Bathgate is Scottish Omnibuses No AA759 (USC 759), an ECW-bodied Bristol LD6G that was new in 1960. Note the advert on the gable end for Red Hackle Whisky. In 1920 Charles Hepburn established Hepburn & Ross, which was owned jointly with Herbert Ross, a fellow soldier who had fought with the Scottish Horse Regiment in Palestine. Hepburn & Ross had a policy of employing ex-servicemen, and their 'Red Hackle' whisky was aimed primarily at the export market. The name is taken from the distinctive red feather worn on the left of the headdress by the Black Watch Regiment, with whom Hepburn had served in the Great War. Although no longer in production, 'Red Hackle' is well remembered, with bottles fetching large sums at auction. I think the bond was in Otago Street, and was owned by Charles Hepburn, who had a Rolls-Royce converted into a delivery van painted black with red coachwork stripes. *transporttreasury.co.uk*

Route 16

Above: **En route to Partick on Sauchiehall Street at the junction of Elmbank Street on 24 June 1958 is Standard hex-dash No 254, followed by Cunarder No 1300. The car on the right is a two-tone Ford Zodiac Mark I, the upmarket version of the Ford Zephyr, which was produced in relatively small numbers between 1954 and 1956.** *David Clarke*

Below: **This is Standard hex-dash No 145 on Keppochhill Road near Carlisle Street on 26 June 1958.** *David Clarke*

GLASGOW CORPORATION ROUTE 17

It is 4 o'clock in the afternoon on 10 June 1959 and the policeman on traffic duty at the junction of Dumbarton Road and Byres Road is having a quiet interlude. There are plenty of pedestrians but a distinct lack of traffic apart from 'Coronation' No 1146. *David Clarke*

Route 17

On 10 October 1954 route 17 between Cambuslang and Anderston Cross or Whiteinch became Cambuslang and Anniesland. Working the route at Glasgow Central station on 6 July 1956 is Standard hex-dash No 169. *David Clarke*

Above: **Standard round-dash No 696 takes on passengers at Bridgeton Cross on the same day. The church in the background is Greenhead parish church.** *David Clarke*

Below: **This is Standard round-dash No 696 at Jordanhill station, also on 6 July 1956. The station opened on 1 August 1887 as part of the Glasgow, Yoker & Clydebank Railway, but the station structure was not completed until 1895. Note the advertisement for Irn-Bru, which was first produced in 1901 in Falkirk under the name 'Strachan's Brew'. In 1946 a change in the law required that the word 'brew' be removed from the name, as the drink is not brewed. The chairman of the company came up with the idea of changing the spelling of both halves of the name, producing the 'Irn-Bru' brand.** *David Clarke*

GLASGOW CORPORATION ROUTE 18

Right: **Standard hex-dash No 109 is seen at the junction of Cambuslang Road and Bothwell Street on 13 July 1956.** *David Clarke*

Route 18

Above: **Route 18 linked Springburn and Rutherglen or Burnside, and seen here is Standard round-dash No 472 at St George's Cross on 26 June 1958. In the background is the Empress Theatre, which was designed by W. B. Whitie and opened on 4 August 1913. In February 1960 it was sold to the Falcon Trust, which renamed it The Falcon Theatre. Alex Frutin purchased it for £40,000 in 1962 and it was reopened as The New Metropole on 22 June. The Scottish comedian Jimmy Logan purchased the theatre in May 1964, renaming it Jimmy Logan's Metropole theatre. In 1974 the building was maliciously burned down and in 1983 was sold to a developer.** *David Clarke*

Right: **A total of 18 Coronation trams were built by Glasgow Corporation in 1940, Nos 1274 to 1291. This is No 1290 on London Road at Greendyke Road on 8 June 1959.** *David Clarke*

Below: **Crossing Dalmarnock Bridge on 10 June 1959 is 'Coronation' No 1159. The bridge was designed by Crouch & Hogg and was opened in 1891. In the background is Dalmarnock's coal-powered power station, which was opened by Glasgow Corporation in two stages between 1920 and 1926. It closed in 1977 and the tower was demolished in 1980. The tram in the far distance is Standard hex-dash No 154.** *David Clarke*

GLASGOW CORPORATION ROUTE 18A

At the junction of Rutherglen Main Street and Farmloan Road on the same day in June 1959 is Standard round-dash No 575. On 3 June 1961 the trams were withdrawn from route 18 and replaced by buses with the same route number. *David Clarke*

Route 18A

This is 'Coronation' No 1275 at Springburn (Hawthorne Street) on 26 June 1958. Note the advert for Sweetheart Stout on the gable end wall. The George Younger Brewery in Alloa started canning Sweetheart Stout in 1958, the cans bearing a picture of Venetia Stevenson. Born in 1938, she moved to America and married Russ Tamblyn in 1956; they divorced in 1957, and she married Don Everly of the Everly Brothers. Her daughter was married to Axl Rose of Guns N' Roses. *David Clarke*

Above: **Route 18A was introduced on 7 August 1955 from Springburn to Shawfield, running alternately with route 18 from Springburn to Bridgeton Cross, then to Shawfield Road at its junction with Rutherglen Road and Glasgow Road. This is Standard round-dash No 575 at Shawfield terminus on 10 June 1959. The tram in the background is 'Coronation' No 1283.** *David Clarke*

Below: **This is Trongate, and in the background is the Tron church with its distinctive steeple and clock, built in the 17th century; it closed as a church in 1952. Approaching the camera in the winter of 1960 is 'Coronation' No 1194. The nearest car is a Ford Zephyr Mark II, and the next car is, I think, a Wolseley 6/90.** *David Clarke*

Route 21

Above: **This is 'Coronation' No 1266 at Elderslie on 7 July 1956. From 10 October 1954 route 21 ran between Elderslie and St Vincent Street.** *David Clarke*

Below: **'Cunarder' No 1380 was photographed in Crookston on 13 July 1956. The Western bus is a Northern Counties-bodied Daimler CVG6,** which was originally with Young's Bus Service Ltd of Paisley. A fleet of around 95 buses were taken over by Western SMT in 1951 and this fleet continued to be the mainstay of bus services in the Paisley area for many years. Route 21 was withdrawn on 11 May 1957. *David Clarke*

Route 22

Above: **In March 1946 route 22, Crookston and St Vincent Street, was extended to Lambhill via Hope Street, Cowcaddens, Garscube Road, Possil Road, Saracen Street and Balmore Road to Strachur Street. Seen on Paisley Road at the junction of Lourdes Avenue on 25 June 1958 is Standard round-dash No 457.** *David Clarke*

Below: **This is Standard hex-dash No 17 at the White City Stadium on 24 June 1958. White City Stadium was built in 1928 as a greyhound track, but also hosted speedway racing with the Glasgow Lions. The club adopted the nickname the Tigers in 1946 and raced at White City intermittently between 1946 and 1968 before moving to Hampden Park in 1969. The White City Stadium was later demolished to make way for the M8 through Glasgow.** *David Clarke*

Above: **This wonderful scene including Standard round-dash No 291 was taken at the junction of Paisley Road West and Moulin Road on 24 June 1958.** *David Clarke*

Below: **This is Standard hex-dash No 178 at Possil Road on 26 June 1958, having just passed under the aqueduct that carried the Port Dundas spur of the Forth & Clyde Canal. The road level was dropped to allow the canal to remain level without locks. The original aqueduct was constructed by Whitworth at the time of the extension of the canal in 1790, and it is still standing next to the 1880s replacement.** *David Clarke*

58 BUSES, TRAMS AND TROLLEYBUSES OF SCOTLAND & IRELAND

'Cunarder' No 1355 stands at Lambhill terminus, also on 26 June 1958. Strachur Street, previously known as Drummond Street, was the Lambhill terminus for route 22. In the background is The Terminus Café where, I am informed, the clippies would exchange their many coins for 10 shilling notes and £1 notes to lighten the load in their heavy money bags. Route 22 was withdrawn on 15 November 1958 and replaced by bus route 54. *David Clarke*

Route 23

No 1237 was photographed on Cambridge Street at Sauchiehall Street on 26 June 1958. The parked car is a Standard Vanguard Phase 1, which was introduced in 1947; more than 174,000 were produced until 1953, when it was replaced by the Vanguard Phase II. The taxi is an Austin FX3, first introduced in 1948; 12,435 were produced until the model was replaced by the FX4 in 1958. *David Clarke*

GLASGOW CORPORATION ROUTE 23

Above: **This is 'Coronation' No 1204 on Duke Street at Shettleston Road on 9 June 1959. The vehicle heading in the opposite direction is a Scammell Scarab, which was produced between 1948 and 1967 and was very popular with British Railways and other companies who made deliveries in built-up areas.** *David Clarke*

Below: **At the junction of Shettleston Road and Kenmore Street on 9 June 1959 is 'Coronation' No 1286. The Savings Bank of Glasgow, an office of which can be seen on the right, opened for business on 30 July 1836, its foundation largely due to Alexander Gray, a Glasgow accountant. The Bank's home was a hospital on Ingram Street, and it quickly established a network of agencies across the city. As Glasgow expanded so did the Bank, and by the late 1930s it had built up a comprehensive branch network across the West of Scotland. In 1976 the Trustees Savings Bank Act resulted in a new regional structure for savings banks, and the Glasgow Savings Bank became the West of Scotland TSB.** *David Clarke*

Above: **Passing Joseph McGreehin's grocer shop at Baillieston, South Scott Street, on the same day is 'Coronation' No 1205.** *David Clarke*

Below: **This is 'Coronation' No 1290 at St George's Cross on 8 September 1959. On 6 November 1960 route 23 was withdrawn and replaced by bus route 60.** *David Clarke*

GLASGOW CORPORATION ROUTE 24

Route 24

Above: **Working route 24 to Anniesland and Langside at Langside Road on 6 July 1956 is Standard hex-dash No 680. This tram, together with 20 others, was built by Glasgow Corporation in 1923-24.** *David Clarke*

Above: **Langside depot was built for tram operations and was opened in 1901. It was converted for bus operations in 1957 and closed in 1984. Passing the depot on 5 July 1956 is 'Coronation' No 1239.** *David Clarke*

Above: **Passing an advertising overload on Victoria Road on the same day is Standard hex-dash No 117.** *David Clarke*

Below: **Standard hex-dash No 286 crosses the junction of Crow Road and Clarence Drive on 6 July 1956.** *David Clarke*

GLASGOW CORPORATION ROUTE 25

Crow Road railway station was opened on 10 October 1896 as part of the Lanarkshire & Dunbartonshire Railway. It closed as part of the 'Beeching Axe' on 6 November 1960, and the main station was demolished in 1970, although the platform still exists. Passing the station on the same day as the previous picture is 'Coronation' No 1241. *David Clarke*

Route 25

It is 2.24pm on 24 June 1958 and the crew of 'Cunarder' No 1330 are taking a break at the terminus of route 25 at Rouken Glen. *David Clarke*

Above: Just a few minutes later, on a wonderfully quiet Rouken Glen Road, we see 'Coronation' No 1223. *David Clarke*

Below: St Rollox station was opened on 1 August 1883, and was comprised of two platforms in a cutting. To the north of the station was the Edinburgh & Glasgow Railway's Sighthill goods yard (now occupied by a Costco cash and carry), and to the south was the Caledonian Railway's St Rollox works. St Rollox station was closed on 14 November 1966 and the station site and cutting have been filled in and landscaped, and now form a footpath. Passing St Rollox station on 24 June 1958 is 'Coronation' No 1223. *David Clarke*

GLASGOW CORPORATION ROUTE 25

Above: **Heading for Carnwadric on Springburn Road at the junction of Carlston Street on 26 June 1958 is Standard hex-dash No 190.** *David Clarke*

Below: **At the busy junction of Springburn Road and Hawthorn Street on 26 June 1958, nearest the camera is Standard round-dash car No 370. Standing in Hawthorn Street working route 33 are Standard hex-dash No 28 and round-dash No 895.** *David Clarke*

Above: **About to pick up a number of passengers on Springburn Road at the junction of Colston Road on 4 June 1959 is Standard hex-dash No 217. The lorry about to overtake is an Albion.** *David Clarke*

Below: **This is Standard hex-dash No 217 on Pollokshaws Road at the junction of Ravenswood Drive on 5 June 1959.** *David Clarke*

Above: **Standard round-dash No 812 is seen at Newlands (Pleasance Street) on the same day. The tower in the background, which has a four-faced clock, is the only surviving fragment of the old Townhouse erected by the 'The Community or Common Council of the Town of Pollokshaws' in 1803. It was built at considerable cost and the debt became a long-term burden to the burgh. It was demolished in 1934. The clock tower is one of the few remnants of the old village to survive the redevelopment of the area in the 1960s.** *David Clarke*

Below: **This is Standard hex-dash No 1050 on Rouken Glen Road on 6 June 1959. The cars in the background are a Hillman Minx and a Morris Minor.** *David Clarke*

On 6 June 1959 route 25 was withdrawn and replaced by bus route 45. Working the route at Bishopbriggs on the last day of service is Standard hex-dash tram No 59. *David Clarke*

Route 26

Above: On 15 August 1943 a new tram route was introduced between Burnside or Rutherglen, Clydebank or Dalmuir West. On 16 November 1958 route 26 became Clydebank or Scotstoun to Farme Cross or Burnside. This is Kilmarnock Bogie No 1094, built by Hurst Nelson in Motherwell in 1927, in Dalmornock Road/Bridgeton Cross on 4 June 1959. The car on the right is an Austin A55 Cambridge, produced between 1957 and 1958. The parked car on the other side of the road is a rather shiny Vauxhall Cresta E. *David Clarke*

Below: At Farme Cross Post Office on 10 June 1959 is 'Coronation' No 1275. *David Clarke*

Above: **The conductor of Kilmarnock Bogie No 1091 is changing the points at Farme Cross Post Office on 10 June 1959.** *David Clarke*

Below: **No 1100 was built by Hurst Nelson in Motherwell in 1927, then in 1940-41 it was rebuilt by Glasgow Corporation. Externally the tram was given altered ends, which were similar to the 'Coronation' trams, and had colour service lights, which were seldom used. Inside it had new stairs and the brown leather seats from a Standard tram. No 1100 gave years of service on shipyard specials from Partick depot, and this view was taken at the junction of Dumbarton Road and Sorley Street on 10 June 1959.** *David Clarke*

GLASGOW CORPORATION ROUTE 27

At the junction of Argyle Street and Virginia Street on 10 August 1959 is Kilmarnock Bogie No 1097. To the left is Lewis's, whose first store was opened in 1856 in Liverpool by entrepreneur David Lewis, as a men's and boys' clothing store, mostly manufacturing his own stock. In 1864 Lewis's branched out into women's clothing. The first Lewis's outside Liverpool opened in nearby Manchester in 1877, and another, by personal suggestion from Joseph Chamberlain, in his new Corporation Street in Birmingham in 1885. A fourth store opened in Sheffield in 1884, but proved unprofitable and closed in 1888. Further new stores were opened in Glasgow (1929), Leeds (1932), Hanley in Stoke-on-Trent (1934) and Leicester (1936). Each Lewis's was generally the largest department store in its locality. On 22 October 1961 the trams terminated at Dalmarnock, and on 2 June 1962 the route was withdrawn.
David Clarke

Route 27

Route 27 was introduced on 15 August 1943 and ran from Springburn to Shieldhall or Renfrew Cross. Here is Standard round-dash No 457 at Paisley Road Toll on 7 July 1956. Less than a year later the service to Renfrew Cross was withdrawn and all the trams terminated at Shieldhall or Hillington Road.
David Clarke

Route 28

Right: **At Renfrew Ferry on 7 July 1956 nearest the camera is Standard hex-dash No 184. The tram behind is a round-dash example, No 909.** *David Clarke*

At Glenfield, also on 7 July 1956, we see Standard hex-dash No 184. Originally, from 15 August 1943, route 28 was for Renfrew Ferry and Spiersbridge, but on 3 April 1949 it became Renfrew and Potterhill to Glenfield. *David Clarke*

GLASGOW CORPORATION ROUTE 28

Left: **The building of Paisley Town Hall, in the background, started in 1879. It was designed by W. H. Lynn of Belfast and features two towers, the taller with four clock faces and an octagonal belfry. The official opening took place on 30 January 1882. Passing on route 28 on the same day as the previous photograph, No 184 is seen again.** *David Clarke*

Above: **This wonderfully tranquil view is Neilston Road at 5.34pm on that same sunny July day. The tram approaching the camera is 'Coronation' No 1282.** *David Clarke*

Left: **This is Standard round-dash No 909 at the railway bridge on Ferry Road on 13 July 1956. The bridge in the background once carried the railway that came from Cardonald via Braehead. Renfrew King's Inch station was near the bridge; renamed from Renfrew Central in 1903, it closed in 1926 and lay derelict until demolished in the 1950s or 1960s.** *David Clarke*

Left: **Standard hex-dash No 167 stands at Renfrew Ferry terminus on the same day.** *David Clarke*

GLASGOW CORPORATION ROUTE 28

Top left: **At Renfrew Cross on 13 July 1956 is Standard hex-dash No 167. In the background is Coia's Cafe and the British Linen Bank. The bank can trace its roots back to 1746 and the initial aim of the company was to promote the linen industry; it issued its first notes in 1747. In 1837 the company acquired the Paisley Banking Company, and in 1906 it formally changed its name to the British Linen Bank. In 1919 it was acquired by Barclays Bank, although it retained a separate board of directors and continued to issue its own bank notes. In 1970 the Bank of Scotland acquired it, but it continued as a separate company until April 2000, when the doors finally closed.** *David Clarke*

Left: **With the Glasgow to Paisley railway line in the background, Standard hex-dash No 182 traverses the single track in Weir Street, also on 13 July 1956.** *David Clarke*

Left: **Approaching the camera on a busy shopping day in Causeyside Street on 13 July 1956 is 'Coronation' No 1280.** *David Clarke*

Bottom left: **Glasgow Corporation built four experimental lightweight four-wheel cars in 1940, Nos 1001 to 1004. None of the cars were quite identical, and No 1003, seen here on Glasgow Road in Paisley at Mansion House Road on 13 July 1956 had an EMB truck with GEC motors and MV controllers. The cars were not particularly well liked and by 1951 all were stationed at Elderslie depot, and were generally used at peak hours only. When the Paisley routes closed they were transferred to Govan, but were scrapped in 1959. Only No 1003 carried large advertisement panels. All tram services in Paisley and Renfrew were abandoned on 11 May 1957.** *David Clarke*

Route 29

Top: Route 29 was introduced on 15 August 1943 from Anderston Cross to Tollcross or Uddingston. On 4 October 1953 the route became Broomhouse or Tollcross and Maryhill or Milngavie. Due to their greater width, the ex-Liverpool 'Green Goddesses' had very limited route capability, but route 29 was one on which they could operate. At the Milngavie terminus on 13 July 1956 is 'Green Goddess' No 1049, and behind it is Standard round-dash car No 315. *David Clarke*

Centre: At Broomhouse terminus on 4 June 1959 are Standard round-dash Nos 862 and 442. The service beyond Tollcross to Broomhouse was abandoned on 6 November 1960. *David Clarke*

Bottom: Ex-Liverpool 'Green Goddess' No 1023 is also seen at Broomhouse terminus on 4 June 1959. Before entering service, the former Liverpool trams had their fenders removed, the windows were altered and they had 'Cunarder' lighting provided. Some later received seats from scrapped Standards as the original seating was high-backed and caused conductor problems. The tram in the background is Standard round-dash No 862. *David Clarke*

GLASGOW CORPORATION ROUTE 29

Left: **This is 'Green Goddess' No 1016 on Milngavie Road at Hillfoot railway station on 13 July 1956. The station was opened in 1900 and is still in use today.** *David Clarke*

Left: **Another 'Green Goddess', No 1010, is seen on Bilsland Drive at Maryhill Road 26 June 1956.** *David Clarke*

Below: **This is Standard round-dash No 398 on Hope Street at Renfrew Street on 26 June 1958. The lorry on the right is a Morris/Austin FE Series III, which was introduced in 1955 and built through to 1958.** *David Clarke*

This is Maryhill Road on 4 June 1959. The aqueduct in the background, which carries the Forth & Clyde Canal, was constructed in 1881, replacing the original one constructed by Whitworth in the 1780s. Nearest the camera is 'Green Goddess' No 1052, and going under the aqueduct is Standard hex-dash No 134. *David Clarke*

Approaching the camera in Trongate on 8 June 1959 is Standard hex-dash No 188, and following is 'Coronation' No 1243. It was around the 1560s that the name Trongate first began to be used, and is derived from a weighbeam erected in the mid-16th century, which was where all goods brought in from the Clyde were weighed and taxed. 'Tron' was the Norman-French-derived Scots term for weighing scales, and the region became known as Trongate. The Tron church in the background, with its distinctive steeple and clock, is the street's best-known landmark, and was substantially redeveloped in the 1980s as the Tron Theatre. The steeple dates from 1631, and the kirk was designed by James Adam and rebuilt after a fire in 1794. *David Clarke*

Working route 29 on Trongate at Glasgow Cross is 'Green Goddess' No 1023, and on the right is 'Cunarder' No 1348. The car in the centre of the view is an Austin A40 Cambridge, and the disappearing estate car to the right is a Standard Vanguard. *David Clarke*

Top: **Passing Tollcross Park on 9 June 1959 is Standard round-dash No 992. Tollcross Park was purchased by Glasgow Corporation for £29,000 and Sir David Richmond, Lord Provost, performed the opening ceremony on 19 June 1897, Queen Victoria's Diamond Jubilee.** *David Clarke*

Centre: **Working route 29 at Anderston Cross, Argyle Street, on 10 June 1959 is 'Green Goddess' No 1056. Note the Guinness advert on the gable end of the building on the right. That company's stature is partly due to its advertising, and the most notable and recognisable series was created by Benson's advertising agency, primarily drawn by the artist John Gilroy in the 1930s and 1940s. Benson's created posters that included phrases such as 'Guinness for Strength', 'Lovely Day for a Guinness', 'Guinness Makes You Strong', 'My Goodness My Guinness' and, most famously, 'Guinness is Good For You'. The posters featured Gilroy's distinctive artwork and more often than not featured animals such as a kangaroo, ostrich, seal, lion and whale.** *David Clarke*

Bottom: **The thing that catches my attention in this view of 'Green Goddess' No 1036 on Argyle Street on 10 August 1959 is the number of people happily walking on the road. David Clarke is also standing in the road to take the photograph.** *David Clarke*

On Hope Street at the junction of Sauchiehall Street on 8 September 1959 is 'Green Goddess' No 1016. These trams seemed to be a bargain buy from Liverpool Corporation, but problems such as lack of bulkheads in the lower deck, leading to drooping platforms, and constant problems with their electric wiring caused their early withdrawal; the last was scrapped in July 1960. *David Clarke*

Route 30

The last extension of the Glasgow tram system was from Knightswood Cross to Blairdardie Canal Bridge, which was opened on 31 July 1949. The extension was a reserved private track, and at the terminus at Blairdardie on 4 June 1959 are Standard hex-dash cars Nos 154 and 9. *David Clarke*

GLASGOW CORPORATION ROUTE 30

Right: **Due to sharp curves causing clearance problems at Parkhead Cross, route 30 was worked entirely by Standard trams. This is hex-dash No 2 in Cambridge Street on 26 June 1958.** *David Clarke*

Below right **Passing Anniesland station on 8 June 1959 is Standard hex-dash No 177. This station was opened as Great Western Road on 20 October 1874 and was renamed Anniesland on 9 January 1931.** *David Clarke*

Below: **In another fine view of the reserved track on Great Western Road, approaching the camera is Standard hex-dash No 124. The houses in the background are part of Glasgow's 'garden city' schemes, which were laid out from 1924.** *David Clarke*

Top: **Glasgow's Queen Street station was officially opened on 18 February 1842. It was built by the Edinburgh & Glasgow Railway and took four years; upon completion the line provided a vital rail link between Glasgow and Edinburgh. Prior to 1909 trains leaving the station via the Cowlairs Tunnel incline had to be hauled up by a rope powered by an engine. With Queen Street station as a backdrop, this is Standard hex-dash No 41 on 9 June 1959.** *David Clarke*

Centre: **This is George Square on the same day, and about to pick up a solitary passenger is Standard hex-dash No 79. The square was named after King George III, a statue of whom was originally intended to occupy the centre of it. However, due to the ill health of the King, a statue of Sir Walter Scott was substituted. George Square was laid out in 1781, and between 1787 and the 1820s it was lined with Georgian townhouses at its east and west ends, together with some hotels.** *David Clarke*

Bottom: **Passing the Beardmore factory on 10 June 1959 is Standard hex-dash car No 40. The Parkhead Forge was established by Reoch Brothers & Co in 1837 and was later acquired by Robert Napier in 1841 to make forgings and iron plates for his new shipyard in Govan. William Beardmore Senior became a partner in the business and, moving to Glasgow, was joined by his brother Isaac and son, William Junior. On the premature death of William Senior, Isaac retired and William Junior became sole partner. He founded William Beardmore & Co in 1886, and by 1896 the works covered an area of 25 acres and was the largest steelworks in Scotland, specialising in the manufacture of steel forgings for the shipbuilding industry of the River Clyde. The Parkhead Forge was nationalised between 1951 and 1954, was acquired by Firth Brown Steels in 1957, and was finally closed in 1976; the land later became The Forge Shopping Centre, which opened in 1988.** *David Clarke*

Passing Newlands School on Springfield Road on the same day in June 1959 is Standard round-dash No 366. The school was built in 1896 and gifted to the school board by Lord Newlands. Tram route 30 was withdrawn and replaced by bus service 58 on 12 March 1960. *David Clarke*

Route 31

Above: **Nos 1141 and 1142 were the prototype 'Coronation' cars and entered service in 1937. They differed from the rest of the class in various ways, including having air-conditioning and internal speaker systems. No 1141 was rebuilt after fire damage in 1949, and in this rebuilt form is seen on 26 August 1959 at Merrylee terminus.** *David Clarke*

Left: **On 8 April 1956 route 31 became Lambhill and Merrylee, and in Pollokshaws Road on 23 June 1958 we see Standard hex-dash No 45.** *David Clarke*

84   BUSES, TRAMS AND TROLLEYBUSES OF SCOTLAND & IRELAND

Left: **Working route 31 on Pollokshaws Road at the junction of Titwood Road on 23 June 1958 is Standard hex-dash No 217.** *David Clarke*

Below: **The last tramcar to Lambhill departed from Union Street at 11.15pm on 5 December 1959 and the route was withdrawn without replacement. This is Standard round-dash No 316 on St Georges Road at Myrtle Street on 26 June 1958.** *David Clarke*

Route 32

Service 32 was introduced on 15 August 1943 and operated from Provanmill to Elderslie. In February 1949 the route became Elderslie and Springburn or Bishopbriggs, and a little over five years later became Crookston and Bishopbriggs. Standard hex-dash No 217 is working the route on Paisley Road West on 24 June 1958. *David Clarke*

Right: **Paisley Road West is a long, wide, straight thoroughfare and was ideally suited for trams, apart from the lack of sufficient loading islands. Working route 32 along the road at the junction of Walmer Crescent on the same day as the previous picture is Standard hex-dash No 128.** *David Clarke*

Right: **On 15 November 1958 route 32 was withdrawn and replaced by bus service 55, and to Bishopbriggs by trams on route 25. At Crookston terminus, also on 24 June 1958, is No 128 again and fellow hex-dash car No 296.** *David Clarke*

Route 33

Route 33 was the only circular tram route in Glasgow and the trams showed Springburn as the destination in both directions. At the junction of Springburn Road and Charles Street on 24 June 1958 is Standard round-dash No 345. *David Clarke*

86 BUSES, TRAMS AND TROLLEYBUSES OF SCOTLAND & IRELAND

On 2 May 1959 the Springburn circular route 33 was withdrawn and was not replaced. Less than a year earlier, at the junction of Maryhill Road and Burnbank Terrace on 26 June 1958, we see Standard hex-dash No 152. *David Clarke*

Other views of Glasgow trams, trolleybuses and buses

A total of 22 'Cunarders', Nos 1370 to 1391, were built by Glasgow Corporation in 1951. This is Renfrew Road on a lovely summer's day in early July 1956 and approaching the camera is 'Cunarder' No 1389. *David Clarke*

Above: **The Great Western Road is Glasgow's longest and straightest road and was originally built as a toll road following an Act of Parliament in 1816. It is lined for much of its length by terraced houses and villas, separated from the road by trees. Approaching the traffic policemen controlling the junction of Byres Road and Great Western Road on 4 June 1959 is Standard hex-dash No 113.** *David Clarke*

Below: **The Kilmarnock Bogie trams, Nos 1090 to 1140, were produced by four builders, Glasgow Corporation, Hurst Nelson of Motherwell, R. Y. Pickering of Wishaw and Brush of Loughborough, and almost exclusively worked on the routes along Dumbarton Road and Argyle Street, where their high passenger capacity was very useful. At the junction of Argyle Street and Sauchiehall Street on 4 June 1959 is No 1095.** *David Clarke*

Right: **On 22 August 1959 'Cunarder' No 1299 passes the entrance to Alexandra Park, which was opened in 1870.** *David Clarke*

Below: **Working route 3 at 1.23pm in the tree-lined Nithsdale Road on 26 August 1959 is Standard hex-dash No 77.** *David Clarke*

Right: **It's 1 September 1959, but looks more like a Scottish summer in Glasgow, making a wonderful background for 'Cunarder' No 1309 at Riddrie. The trams would cease between Riddrie and Scotstoun two months later on 1 November.** *David Clarke*

GLASGOW CORPORATION

Top: **During 1937 Glasgow Corporation took delivery of 25 Weymann-bodied Daimler COG6s, Nos 510 to 534 (BGA 76 to 100). Working route 7A to Kilmorie Drive is No 514 (BGA 79).** *Phil Sposito*

Upper centre: **Albion Motors Ltd of Scotstoun, Glasgow, was established in 1899 and quickly became Scotland's most important commercial vehicle manufacturer, producing lorries and buses that sold in greater numbers overseas than they did in their own country. The Albion Venturer CX19 was introduced in 1938 with a choice of Gardner or Albion diesel engines, but after the war only Albion engines were offered. With a production life spanning 11 years, interrupted for four years by the Second World War, the CX19 became Albion's longest-lived and most successful double-deck chassis design, especially overseas. Two cities ran sizeable fleets, Glasgow and Sydney, but by 1961 all of the Glasgow examples had gone. This is No 814 (DGB 462), one of a batch of 20 Pickering-bodied Albion Venture CX19s new in 1940. The delivery van is working for the Vindanda Laundry of Lenzie Road, Kirkintilloch, which was still in existence in the early 1970s.** *Phil Sposito*

Lower centre: **Fifty Crossley-bodied AEC Regent IIIs, Nos A21 to A70 (FYS 121 to FYS 170), were delivered to Glasgow Corporation in 1948, built on 9612E-type chassis with fluid flywheels, air-operated pre-selective gearboxes and air brakes. Representing this batch is No A66 (FYS 166). Long John whisky dates back to the early 20th century, and is made at the Tormore distillery; it is a blend of 48 malts, including Laphroaig and Highland Park, which definitely influence its distinctive taste.** *Phil Sposito*

Bottom: **Working route 16 to Balornock East is No A199 (FYS 383), a Weymann-bodied AEC Regent III that was part of a batch of 100 delivered during 1951. The advertisement board in the right background is for Usher's export ale. Ushers began brewing in Trowbridge, Wiltshire, in 1824, and the brewery remained in the Usher family until 1960, when the company merged with Watney Mann.** transporttreasury.co.uk

Above: **Between 25 February and 29 June 1949 a total of 34 three-axle BUT 9641Ts, Nos TB 1 to 34 (FYS 701 to 734), were delivered to Glasgow Corporation, and working route 102 to Polmadie is No TB 13 (FYS 713). The High Street routes were No 101 and 102, which were at times very busy, and the majority of the trolleybuses used on them were these three-axle types. No TB 13 entered service on 8 April 1949 and was among the last of the 34 to be withdrawn, on 30 April 1966. Route 101 started on 6 November 1949 and the last day of trolleybus operations was 20 April 1966. Route 102 started on 3 April 1949 and ceased operations on 30 April 1966.** *Phil Sposito*

Above: **During 1955 a batch of 25 Leyland PD2/25s were purchased new. Bodied by Alexander to a Weymann design and 7ft 6in wide, they had fluid flywheels, a pneumo-cyclic gearbox with two-pedal control, and a floor-mounted pedestal gear change. Numbered L 24 to 48 (FYS 647 to 671), this is No L37 (FYS 660), demoted from service to trainer duties.** *Phil Sposito*

GLASGOW CORPORATION

Top: **Working route 16A to Balornock East is No A300 (FYS 606), one of a batch of 49 AEC Regent Vs new in 1955 with Alexander bodywork to a Weymann design. This batch had D2RV6G-type chassis, Gardner 6LW engines, fluid flywheels, spring-operated pre-selective gearboxes and vacuum brakes.** transporttreasury.co.uk

Centre: **Before the end of Burlingham's independence there was an important development with trolleybuses as Glasgow Corporation ordered a batch of ten single-deck 50-seaters on BUT RETB1 chassis. These were Burlingham's only electrically powered single-deckers and the longest single-deckers yet seen in Britain. They were numbered TBS12 to 21 (FYS 987 to 996) and were delivered between 22 October and 12 November 1958. They were 35 feet long and ran exclusively on the suburban route 108 between Shieldhall and Paisley Road Toll. This is No TBS15 (FYS 990), which was licensed on 4 November 1958, and route 108 began trolleybus operations on the 15th, replacing tram route 12. The Linthouse and Shieldhall service was withdrawn on 14 November 1964, and the last day of trolleybus operations on route 108 was 4 March 1967, the day that No TBS15 was withdrawn.** *Phil Sposito*

Bottom: **On the first day of December 1958 the last two trolleybuses purchased by Glasgow Corporation entered service on route 108. These were Nos TBS20 and 21, and seen on a National Trolleybus Association Tour of the system is the latter (FYS 996). Who remembers Pink Stamps? They were particularly popular during the mid-1960s and early 1970s together with Green Shield stamps.** *Phil Sposito*

Right: **From July 1957 through to November 1958 a total of 90 BUT 9613Ts with Crossley bodywork were delivered to Glasgow Corporation, and became the mainstay of routes 105, 106 and 107. Working route 106 in August 1966 is No TB50 (FYS 811). In the background is the Lyceum, which was designed by McNair & Elder and opened in December 1938, originally seating 2,600. It replaced the original Lyceum Theatre, which had opened in 1899 and burned down in 1937.** *David Clarke*

Centre: **Trolleybus operations on route 105 began on 5 July 1953 between Queen's Cross and Clarkston, replacing part of tram route 13. Working the route in the late autumn of 1966 is No TB65 (FYS 826). This was the last trolleybus route to operate in Scotland, being withdrawn on 27 May 1967 and replaced by bus route 66.** *Phil Sposito*

Below: **This excellent view of No TB67 (FYS 828) was taken in August 1966. New in the first weeks of January 1958, this trolleybus survived until the end of the system in Glasgow on 27 May 1967.** *David Clarke*

GLASGOW CORPORATION

Above: Working route 105 on a rather gloomy day in the late autumn of 1966 is No TB70 (FYS 831). On the left is an Austin FX4 taxi; it is remarkable to think that this model has been around since 1958. The first FX4 was fitted with a 2,178cc Austin diesel engine and a Borg-Warner automatic transmission. In 1961 the manual transmission from the Austin Gypsy was available as an option, and from 1962 the Austin 2,199cc petrol engine was available. However, almost all FX4s were fitted with a diesel engine, and until the mid-1970s most had manual transmission. *Phil Sposito*

Below: Working route 105 to Queen's Cross in August 1966 is No TB101 (FYS 862), which was delivered on 1 July 1958 and entered service at the end of that month. Only four months after this photograph was taken it was withdrawn after a service life of just over eight years. The car in the background is a Ford Zephyr/Zodiac Mark II, which was produced between 1956 and 1962. *David Clarke*

Right: Working route 53 between Springburn and Shieldhall in the winter of 1966 is No L329 (SGD 329), a Leyland PD2/24 new in 1960 and bodied by Glasgow Corporation to an Alexander design. Between 1956 and 1960 a total of 300 Leyland PD2/24s were purchased and all were 8 feet wide and had fluid flywheels, a pneumo-cyclic gearbox with two-pedal control, and a floor-mounted pedestal gear change. *transporttreasury.co.uk*

Above: Between 1960 and 1961 Glasgow Corporation took delivery of 140 Leyland PD3/2s, one of which, No L398, was a PD3A/2. Twenty-five, Nos L349 to 373, had bodywork by Glasgow Corporation, and the remainder were bodied by Alexander. Working route 35 between North Carntyne and Balornock in the winter of 1966 is No L437 (SGD 439). Nos L349 to L488 were delivered with Albion Titan radiator badges, and were fitted with air-operated passenger doors. *transporttreasury.co.uk*

Right: **The first Leyland PDR1/1, No LA1 (FYS 998), which had a very boxy Alexander body, was delivered to Ibrox depot and entered service on 15 December 1958 for evaluation. During 1962 a total of 150 Alexander-bodied PDR1/1s were delivered, with Leyland O.600 130bhp engines and an electric gear change on the steering column. They also had a three-piece hood, of which only the centre section opened, and all were delivered with Albion Atlantean badges front and rear. This is one of the 1962 Leyland PDR1/1s, No LA114 (SGD 692), working route 60 to Shettleston.**

The lorry in the background is delivering for Wells Brimtoy. Brimtoy started in 1914 and later merged with Wells. Around 1938 the company was producing tinplate toys at a factory on Stirling Road in Walthamstow. By 1949 the factory was employing 700 workers and the tinplate toys were extremely popular. However, for most model enthusiasts it is the buses, trolleybuses and coaches that have the greatest appeal. Production ceased in 1965 and today many of the models are purchased for well over £100. *transporttreasury.co.uk*

Below: **Just about to cross Glasgow Bridge working route 4 to Drumoyne in June 1972 is No LA238 (CYS 584B), an Alexander-bodied Leyland PDR1/1 delivered in February 1965. The store in the background is Paisleys Ltd, a long-established Glasgow tailor and outfitter founded in the late 19th century. The company's department store on the corner of Jamaica Street and Clyde Street was particularly popular with parents shopping for school uniforms for their children. The store was acquired by Sir Hugh Fraser in the 1980s, who traded there briefly and renamed the store 'Sir Hugh'. The building has since been demolished and is now a hotel complex.**

Belfast Corporation

Belfast's first trams arrived in 1872, horse-drawn and operated by the Belfast Street Tramways Company. The system was purchased by Belfast Corporation on 1 January 1905 and electrified during that year, using overhead wires.

In 1926 Belfast Corporation began to operate buses when six AEC 413s were purchased new. By 1928 a total of 16 independent operators had been taken over, bringing to the fleet 51 varied makes of single-deck buses. Between 1930 and 1935 29 double-deck buses were purchased, together with 30 Dennis Lancets.

In 1938 seven pairs of each make of trolleybus available at the time were purchased for tram replacement trials. This resulted in the purchase of 88 AEC 664Ts and 14 Sunbeam W trolleybuses, which were placed in service between 1941 and 1943.

During 1944 Belfast Corporation took delivery of a number of Harkness utility-bodied Daimler CWA6s. The majority were rebuilt by Harkness in 1953, and working service 25 in Donegall Square in September 1963 is No 209 (GZ 1877). No 209 was withdrawn during 1969 and sold for scrap in December of that year. The bus in the background is No 577 (577 EZ), an MH Cars-bodied Daimler CRG6LX that was new in December 1962. It was renumbered 2577 when it passed to Citybus in April 1973, and unfortunately was destroyed on 22 March 1977.

BELFAST CORPORATION

During the war years Belfast received 30 Bedford OWBs, seven Guy Arabs and 43 Daimler CWA6s. The first buses purchased after the war were 40 Daimler CVA6s, which entered service between 1946 and 1947. Buses and trolleybuses continued to be bought new, but in 1953, to speed up the tramway replacement programme, 100 Daimler CWA6s were purchased from London Transport. Also purchased second-hand were 11 Sunbeam trolleybuses from Wolverhampton. The London Daimlers entered service unaltered, but after the trams were withdrawn in 1954 they were rebodied during 1955 and 1956. One more trolleybus, a Sunbeam, was purchased in 1958. Also purchased in that year was an AEC Bridgemaster, which was joined over the next three years by a Leyland Atlantean and a Dennis Loline. Belfast Corporation decided to introduce the Daimler Fleetline to its fleet, even though the make had not been trialled, and it became the standard double-deck bus for many years.

In May 1968 the trolleybuses ceased to operate, and a mixed bag of single-deckers arrived between 1969 and 1970, consisting of 18 Daimler Roadliners, 18 AEC Swifts and 30 single-deck Fleetlines. For a number of reasons, in April 1973 the Belfast Corporation fleet became Citybus, a sister company of Ulsterbus, and took over an operational fleet of around 350 buses. The Bristol RE became the company's standard bus; the last was delivered in 1984, by which time the former Corporation fleet had been largely withdrawn.

During 1954 Belfast Corporation took delivery of 23 Harkness-bodied BUT 9641T trolleybuses, numbered 212 to 234 (OZ 7314 to 7336). Also seen in Donegall Square in September 1963 is No 225 (OZ 7327). The car behind it is a Triumph Renown, which was distinctively styled; the body was built by Mulliner of Birmingham using the traditional coachbuilder's method of sheet metal over a wooden frame. The panels were not made of steel, but from aluminium, but by the early 1950s aluminium had become expensive and probably hastened the demise of the model.

Top: **This is No 214 (GZ 1882), another of the utility-bodied Daimler CWA6s new in 1944. After accident damage it was rebuilt in 1950, and thus looks different from the Harkness rebuilds of 1953. This view of No 214 heading for Mount Pottinger was taken in September 1963. Note the unusual location of the advertisement for McKibbins Rum.**

Centre: **Working service 30 to Bloomfield is No 234 (OZ 7336), a Harkness bodied BUT 9641T trolleybus new in 1954. The Belfast trolleybus system began operation on 28 March 1938, and at its height there was a fleet of 245 trolleybuses, which made it the second-largest system in the UK after London. It was the only one in Ireland and ceased operations on 12 May 1968.**

Bottom: **During 1947 Belfast received a large order of Harkness/Park Royal-bodied Daimler CVA6s, and representing this batch in Donegall Square in September 1963, is No 248 (GZ 4002). Many of this batch, including this vehicle, were withdrawn from service in 1964.**

Above: **Between October 1953 and March 1954 Belfast purchased from North of Leeds 100 former London Transport Daimler CWA6s, bodied by Duple, Park Royal and Brush. They were intended for tram replacement and entered service as acquired. The trams ceased on 10 February 1954, and during the next two years all 100 buses were rebodied by Harkness. Seen in Donegall Square in September 1973 is No 505 (GXV 790). Originally bodied by Brush, it had entering service with London Transport in April 1945 as No D59; it was withdrawn in October 1953 and sold to North of Leeds, which quickly sold it Belfast Corporation. No 505 remained in service until 1970.**

Below: **Between 1958 and 1961 Belfast Corporation purchased an AEC Bridgemaster, a Leyland PDR1/1 and a Dennis Loline with the objective of determining the future fleet replacement. Even though the type had not been on trial, the Corporation decided to purchase Daimler Fleetlines with bodywork to an Alexander design built by MH Cars in Belfast, which later became MH Coachworks. A total of 151 Daimler CRG6LXs and three Leyland PDR1/1s were built in Belfast, and a further two CRG6LXs were purchased by Bournemouth. The first MH-bodied Daimlers were new in August 1962, and representing the early batch is 567 EZ, originally No 567, and renumbered 2567 in the Belfast Citybus fleet in April 1973. This view was taken in June 1975 at Donegall Quay, with the River Lagan in the background. The bus was destroyed in Falls Park Depot on 18 January 1979 and sold for scrap the following month.**

Above: **Crossing Queen's Bridge in June 1975 is 615 EZ, originally No 615 and renumbered 2615 by Citybus in April 1973. This MH-bodied Daimler CRG6LX was new in May 1963 and was scrapped after being seriously damaged in September 1979. The car to the left is an Austin Maxi; this was the last production car designed by Alec Issigonis and was launched in Oporto, Portugal, on 24 April 1969. The price in that year was £979, and the last Maxi rolled off the production line in Cowley in July 1981.**

Below: **The MH-bodied Daimler CRG6LXs were still arriving during 1964, and new in February of that year was 658 EZ, seen here in Oxford Street in June 1975 as Citybus No 2658. A little over a year later the bus was destroyed, and had been scrapped by November 1976. MH Cars, MH Coachworks and Potters took over building from each other until the business became Walter Alexander & Sons (Belfast) Ltd, which was jointly owned by Alexander's at Falkirk and the Northern Ireland Transport Holding Company.**

Above: **During 1969 two batches of Potters-bodied single-deck buses were delivered, with 18 vehicles in each. The first 18 were Daimler SRC6s, and the remainder were AEC Swifts. The latter were new in May 1969, and one of them, Citybus No 2756 (756 UZ), is seen working route 16 on Queen's Bridge in June 1975. All of the Daimler SRC6s were withdrawn by August 1977, and the Swifts lasted a little longer, all having gone by November 1979.**

Below: **Thirty Daimler CRG6LX/33s with bodies by Alexander (Belfast) were delivered between December 1969 and February 1970, and seen in Donegall Square East is one of three new in that first month. Numbered 2780 in the Citybus fleet, AOI 780 was still on the fleet strength in 1981, but was destroyed in Ardoyne Depot in August 1981. The buses in the background are Alexander (Belfast)-bodied Bristol RELL6Gs, which were purchased new by Citybus from mid-1976 for many years.**

A batch of 20 Daimler CRG6LX-33s bodied by Alexander (Belfast) began to arrive in October 1972. Five did not arrive until April 1973, and these were Nos 2863, 2865, 2870, 2871 and 2872 (EOI 4863, EOI 4865 and EOI 4870 to 4872). No 2865, seen here at Donegall Quay in June 1975, remained in service until March 1989. The building in the background is the Custom House. In its heyday Belfast was a very important port, with only London and Liverpool collecting more duty from goods passing through. The Custom House was built in 1857 to a design by Sir Charles Lanyon (1813-89) in the High Italian Renaissance or 'Palazzo' style, and it is claimed to be the finest neoclassical building in Belfast. The area in front of the Custom House had been used as a dock for lime and salt, but in recent years has been transformed into a multi-purpose event area hosting arts festivals and performance events.

Coras Iompair Eireann

Coras Iompair Eireann (CIE) was formed in January 1945 with the amalgamation of two bus fleets belonging to Dublin United Transport and Great Southern Railways. The combined fleet was 688 buses, and the new company also had responsibility for the trams in Dublin as well as the rail network of GSR.

Right: Between 1948 and 1953 a total of 361 CIE-bodied Leyland Tigers entered CIE service. Seen in Dublin in September 1963 is No P95 (ZH 6365), a CIE-bodied Leyland OPS3/1 new in June 1949.

Below: Between April 1948 and July 1949 CIE purchased 150 all-Leyland Titans, Nos R291 to R440, and with their arrival the last Dublin trams ran in July 1949. This is No R393 (ZJ 1353), an all-Leyland PD2/3 new in July 1949 seen in O'Connell Street in Dublin in September 1963. The approaching bus on the left is No R344 (ZH 4493), another all-Leyland PD2/3 new in November 1948. The bus outside the Savoy is No RA24 (CYI 659), a CIE-bodied Leyland PD3/2 new in March 1959. The film showing at the cinema is *Two for the Seesaw* with Robert

Opposite: The first Great Northern Railway (Ireland) bus service began on 29 January 1929 between Drogheda railway station and West Street using three Leyland Lions. A total of nine bus companies were taken over in 1929, and by the end of the year the fleet had grown to 64 buses. In 1937 the first double-deckers were purchased, 21 buses being designed and built by the GNR at Dundalk. In 1948 came the largest purchase of new buses, when a total of 50 entered service, three of which being built by the GNR. This is ZH 3925, a Park Royal-bodied AEC Regal new to the GNR in October 1948. Originally numbered 426 by the GNR, it became CIE No A426 in October 1958, and this view was taken at Carlingford in September 1963, a few months before its withdrawal from service.

104 BUSES, TRAMS AND TROLLEYBUSES OF SCOTLAND & IRELAND

Right: Mitchum and Shirley MacLaine. During 1952 the GNR took delivery of four Leyland PSU1/9s with Saunders Roe (SARO) bodies; they were the only centre-entrance buses in the GNR and CIE fleets. Numbered 225 to 228 (ZO 3762, ZO 4076, ZO 4401 and IY 3890), all four passed to CIE in October 1958, and seen in Drogheda in September 1963 is the now renumbered U226 (ZO 4076). SARO, of Beaumaris, Anglesey, had its origins in boatbuilding, but had become involved with the manufacture of aircraft during the Second World War. During the early 1950s the company diversified into building bus bodies and secured a large order from London Transport for double-deckers on RT chassis. The SARO bodies were built mainly from aluminium instead of the usual steel and wood used by most builders at that time; this gave a weight saving of almost a ton, and the bodies did not suffer from as much corrosion as those made from steel, but their initial purchase price was greater.

Below: Another of the SARO-bodied Leyland PSU1/9's, No U227 (ZO 4401), is also seen in Drogheda in the same month. On the left is No AR295 (IY 5937), one of 17 Park Royal-bodied AEC Regent IIIs purchased by the GNR in 1948, and originally numbered 289 to 298 and 433 to 439; note its quite extensive bodywork damage.

Right: **In 1953 CIE purchased six Leyland OPD2/1s, which were bodied by CIE as double-deck coaches specifically for the service between Dublin city centre and the airport. They were numbered R541 to R546 (ZO 6960 to ZO 6963, and ZO 9341 and ZO 9342) and had 50 seats, a centre staircase and entrance, and a large walk-in luggage compartment behind the back axle. This picture of No R541 (ZO 6960), taken at Dublin Airport in September 1963, shows suitcases being loaded into the luggage compartment. The airport service was converted to single-deck operation in 1964 and these Titans were rebuilt as rear-platform 68-seat half-cab buses. All were withdrawn from a long service life in September 1974, and No R541 survives in preservation.**

Below: **A total of 38 CIE-bodied rear-entrance Leyland PSU1/13s were delivered in the early months of 1954. They were Nos U51 to U88 (ZO 6922 to 6950), and seen in Dublin in September 1963 is No U61 (ZO 6932). Throughout the mid-1960s all these buses were re-built, 29 to dual-doorway and nine to front-entrance. Most were withdrawn from service by 1972, but a number survived as driver trainers until 1980.**

Above: In the early months of 1954 CIE briefly took on loan Southdown's Harrington-bodied Leyland PSU1/15 MUF 430. As a result 50 coaches were built by CIE to a design very much resembling the Harrington coach body; mounted on Leyland PSU1/15 chassis, they were the only coaches to be built by CIE with centre entrances. The first six, Nos U1 to U6, entered service in July and August 1954, and representing this batch is No U6 (ZO 6877), in Dublin in September 1963.

Below: The last new buses for the Great Northern Railway fleet were 33 AEC Regal IV buses and coaches bodied by Park Royal. Seen in Arklow in September 1963 is ZV 773, which had coach bodywork originally with a rear entrance. It was originally numbered 334 in the GNR fleet, renumbered AU334 by CIE, later rebuilt by CIE with a front entrance, and withdrawn from a long service life in November 1973.

Above: **ZY 1165** was another of the GNR Park Royal-bodied AEC Regal IVs, this time with bus bodywork, new in October 1955. It was rebuilt with a front entrance by CIE, and was withdrawn from service in August 1973. The last day of operations for the GNR buses was 30 September 1958, when the entire road fleet passed to CIE together with the surviving rail network in the Republic of Ireland.

Below: **This is No R601 (JRI 31)**, a CIE-bodied Leyland OPD2/10 new in November 1955, photographed in Dublin in May 1974, just a few months before withdrawal from service.

Above: In Cork in May 1974 is No R702 (BIK 302), another CIE-bodied Leyland OPD2/10 new in January 1957. Note the bilingual final destination (Togher/Tochar).

Below: Working service 12 to Palmerston Park in O'Connell Street in September 1963 is a further example, No R711 (BIK 311), new in January 1957. A total of 225 CIE-bodied Leyland OPD2/10s entered service between January 1956 and October 1958. Some were modified with platform doors so that they could be used on rural services, and the last of these attractive buses were withdrawn from service in mid-1976. The Dalkey-bound bus is No RA4 (CYI 639), one of the first CIE-bodied Leyland PD3/2s to enter service in March 1959. Beside it is No R307 (ZH 4456), an all-Leyland PD2/3 new in July 1948.

Above: Seen in Waterford in May 1974 is No R741 (OIK 937), another CIE-bodied Leyland OPD2/10, new in June 1957. The car on the left is a Humber Sceptre, which was the luxury variant of the Hillman Hunter, first introduced in September 1967. Initially produced at Ryton-on-Dunsmore, Coventry, between 1967 and 1969, production was transferred to Linwood in 1969, where it remained until 1976, when the last Humber finally rolled off the production line and into the history books. During its time in production the vehicle's appearance changed very little.

Below: Another example of the same model, No R788 (OIK 984), new in January 1958, is seen in Waterford in May 1974. It was withdrawn from service in August 1977 and sold to a school in Limerick in August 1979. It later passed into preservation and has been restored in the CIE green livery. This view was taken at Meagher's Quay, and the destination display is completely in English.

Above: Crossing O'Connell Bridge over the River Liffey in May 1974 is No R804 (CYI 606), a CIE-bodied Leyland OPD2/10 new in April 1958. O'Connell Bridge is the main bridge over the Liffey in Dublin, and was designed by James Gandon between 1791 and 1794. In 1882 it was widened to its current state and now forms part of O'Connell Street. The bridge is unique in Europe because it is wider than it is long.

Below: By 1974 the Dublin city centre terminus of the trunk Dun Laoghaire routes 7A, to Sallynoggin, and 8, to Dalkey, had moved from O'Connell Street to Eden Quay, on the north bank of the River Liffey. No RA10 (CYI 645) is turning from Eden Quay and heading south across O'Connell Bridge. This bus was new in March 1959 and, after an accident in February 1976, was withdrawn and later scrapped. The Corinthian cinema on the right was designed by T. F. McNamara, with internal alterations to the auditorium in the 1930s by Jones & Kelly. At some point it acquired a modern façade when the auditorium was split into several smaller cinemas. It was demolished in late 2002 to make way for a commercial development.

Routes 7A to Sallynoggin and 8 to Dalkey provided a very frequent service south-eastwards from Dublin city centre, running close to the coast as far as Dun Laoghaire before splitting to their separate destinations. The first picture shows No RA12 (CYI 647), a CIE-bodied Leyland PD3/2 new in March 1959, leaving the city centre for Dalkey in September 1963, while in the second we see No RA13 (CYI 648) crossing O'Connell Bridge working service 7A in May 1974. These impressive double-deckers were the mainstay of these trunk bus routes, and the last two in service were Nos RA33 and RA95, withdrawn at Clontarf Depot in April 1982, both having achieved more than 20 years of service.

Above: **Heading for Drimnagh along O'Connell Street in September 1963 is No RA117 (HZA 242), another of the impressive semi-automatic-gearbox CIE-bodied Leyland PD3/2s, this particular bus being new in December 1960. Travelling behind it is No R718 (BIK 318), a CIE-bodied Leyland OPD2/10 that was new in February 1957.**

Below: **The three AEC Regent Vs new in June 1961, Nos AA1 to AA3 (HZA 278 to 280), were an unusual purchase for CIE, and were allocated to Waterford Depot specifically to operate the bus service that had replaced trains on the Tramore line. The Waterford & Tramore Railway was unique in Ireland because it was unconnected to any other. The trains made the journey of 7¼ miles on the 5ft 3in-gauge line from Railway Square, Tramore, to Manor Street station (also known as Railway Square) in Waterford – there were no intermediate stations. The line opened for business on 15 September 1853 and was operated independently until 1925, when it became part of the Great Southern Railways. Despite considerable local opposition, the last trains ran to Tramore on 31 December 1960. Tramore is a popular seaside destination and at the time there was much concern about how replacement buses would cope with summer the crowds. These AEC buses, introduced at the beginning of the summer 1961 season, were fitted with additional space for luggage. This view of No AA3 was taken in May 1974.**

Above: A total of 26 CIE-bodied Leyland L2s were delivered between August and December 1961, and a further 144 were bodied at Spa Road Works between 1962 and 1964, the last two entering service in January 1965. Representing the E Class Leyland L2 is No E48 (CZA 708), seen here in Naas, County Kildare, in May 1974.

Below: Entering service between 1962 and 1964 were 23 CIE-built luxury coaches on Leyland Worldmaster chassis with unusual bodywork designed by David Ogle & Associates. This is No WT15 (HZD 594) on extended tour work in a hotel car park in Killarney in May 1974. The bodies had steel frames and panelling, which caused them to be very heavy, and they were all withdrawn in 1970 and 1971 and the chassis rebodied by Van Hool in Belgium; No WT15 was rebodied in June 1970, and renumbered WVH14.

David Ogle founded his design consultancy in Letchworth in 1954 and the company became involved with transport design and small car production in 1959. Three years later its founder was killed in a car crash. The company designed, among others, the Scimitar GTE of 1968, the Bond Bug, the Reliant Robin, the Plaxton Panorama 1 of 1964, the Plaxton Panorama Elite of 1968, the Duple Dominant in 1972, and the Plaxton Paramount range of coach bodywork.

BUSES, TRAMS AND TROLLEYBUSES OF SCOTLAND & IRELAND

Opposite top: This is No PL12 (NZO 12), a Plaxton coach-bodied Leyland PSU3A/4R new to CIE in April 1969. It is in CIE Coach Tours livery, but is actually on bus work and operating the 18.00 journey from Galway south to Lisdoonvarna. It is approaching the village of Ballyvaughan, passing the remains of Shan Muckinish on the edge of Pouldoody Bay. The castle is a Tower House and Bawn, which was occupied/founded in 1580 by O'Loghlen.

Main picture: No C201 (EZH 210) is a CIE-bodied Leyland PSU3/4R new in May 1966. Spa Road Works began to produce a second large group of Leopards, the C Class, from 1965 onwards; their bodies were supplied in kit form by Metal Sections of Oldbury and were assembled and furnished in Dublin. A total of 146 C Class buses entered service in 1965, and a further 114 arrived in 1966. Some were fitted out as 40-seater tour coaches, others as 45-seater express coaches, with the majority being either 45-seat or 53-seat service buses. This very well-laden example is operating the 18.00 journey from Galway to Carna and is seen running along the north shore of Galway Bay passing through Spiddal. Spiddal is particularly known for Coláiste Chonnacht, a language college established in 1906 by the Gaelic League to train teachers in the Irish language, which moved here after acquiring premises in 1910. Today the college runs courses for students keen to learn about the Irish language, culture and traditions.

CORAS IOMPAIR EIREANN

Right: **This view of No PL33 (NZO 33) was taken in May 1974, while it was operating an extended tour to the County Kerry and Killarney areas and was parked at Limerick Depot overnight. No PL33 had Plaxton bodywork with coach seating, but was altered to dual-purpose seating in 1982.**

Right: **This is No R915 (NZE 624), a Leyland PD3A/6 new in February 1965 with its distinctive Park Royal bodywork.** As increasing numbers of underfloor-engine single-deck buses entered service, CIE scrapped many of the P Class half-cab Leyland Tigers, which were unsuitable for driver-only operation. A shortage of double-deckers was relieved by using mechanical components from these P Class vehicles as part of new Leyland Titans, for which the bodywork was supplied in kit form from Park Royal, and assembled in the former GNR works at Dundalk in 1964 and 1965. Twenty-six such buses (Nos R901 to R926) were built and designated as Leyland PD3A/6s, the only such examples. This view was taken in May 1974 as the bus crossed O'Connell Bridge – not, in my opinion, the most attractive design.

Below: **Three interesting buses saw service with CIE in 1964, when the Transport Departments of Bolton, Liverpool and Glasgow loaned it one bus each for six months for service trials in Dublin and Cork. In each case the chassis was the Leyland Atlantean,** but each had a different body design. The resulting experiences were assessed in detail prior to the building of the next generation of Irish double-deckers from late 1966 onwards. The outcome was the D Class double-deckers, and CIE's first D Class Atlantean, No D4, entered service in Dublin on 29 November 1966 on routes 19 and 19A; a further seven examples were in service by Christmas that year. This is No D223 (VZI 223), a CIE/MSL-bodied Leyland PDR1/1 new in June 1969, leaving the town of Maynooth, about 15 miles west of Dublin, and heading back to the city centre showing the common bilingual display An Lar/City Centre.

Top: **Working service 2 in Cork in May 1974 is No D301 (VZI 301), a CIE/MSL-bodied Leyland PDR1A/1 new in September 1969. The new Atlanteans featured forced-air ventilation and sealed windows on both decks, but lack of air led to the design being revised to include eight windows with top slider vents (two per side on each deck), this being standard from No D132 onwards, and quickly fitted to the earlier buses.**

Centre: **This is No D331 (VZI 331), another CIE/MSL-bodied Leyland PDR1A/1 new in June 1970, and seen in Waterford in May 1974. Note the destination display, which has been reduced to a single line, in complete contrast to the very full displays on Nos R741 and R788 seen in Waterford on the same day in 1974 (see page 109). The blue van on the left is, I think, a Fiat 850.**

Below: **No M47 (47 IK) is a CIE/MSL-bodied Leyland PSU5/4R new in August 1971, and is seen in 1980 at Carraroe working the 16.20 journey from Galway to Lettermullen, which is on an island, and the bus has to traverse causeways and bridges to reach it. The M Class vehicles were introduced to the CIE fleet in the summer of 1971, the last of the fleet of 213 being delivered in June 1973. The class consisted of 53 coaches, 140 dual-purpose buses and 20 tour buses with higher windscreens and no destination equipment.**

Above: CIE's demand for buses was not enough to keep Spa Road Works in full production, so in 1973 Van Hool teamed up with Thomas McArdle Ltd of Dundalk to form Van Hool McArdle, which leased the works and took over 248 CIE staff. During the next five years the company produced just under 800 buses, more than half of which were Leyland Atlanteans and Bedford SB5s for CIE. Van Hool McArdle introduced a very different double-deck body design, the first Leyland Atlantean entering service in 1973. Leyland AN68s Nos D603 to D840 all received Van Hool McArdle bodywork, and seen in Dun Laoghaire is No D818 (818 NIK), a Leyland AN68/1R new in May 1976. The Atlanteans proved mechanically unreliable, with customer support from British Leyland also proving to be a problem. In order to alleviate the mechanical problems, CIE replaced some of the Leyland 600 (9.8-litre) and 680 (11.1-litre) engines with new DAF DK1160 (11.6-litre) engines derived from the original Leyland 680. No D818 received a DAF engine and was renumbered DF818, remaining in service until June 1994.

Main picture: This is No M173 (173 IK), a CIE/MSL coach-bodied Leyland PSU5/4R new in January 1972. In January 1979 the bus was renumbered MG173, indicating that it was fitted with a General Motors engine. In this view it is in 'Expressway' livery and is seen approaching Westport in County Mayo operating the 08.45 journey from Achill Island

to Ballina via Westport and Castlebar. Achill Island is connected to the mainland by a swing bridge named after the 19th-century Irish social campaigner Michael Davitt, who officially opened it in 1887. The present-day bridge only dates from 2008.

Lough Swilly

The Londonderry & Lough Swilly Railway commenced public service in 1863, and by the end of the century had established a network of narrow-gauge lines linking Derry and Letterkenny. In the late 1920s privately owned buses began to compete with the trains, so in 1929 Barr of Buncrana, with four buses, was taken over. Five new Leylands were purchased in 1930 and a further nine buses were acquired with the takeover of four more Donegal-based operators.

As the railway network diminished, the bus fleet increased, and in 1946 the first of a fleet of post-war half-cab single-deckers entered service. A year later saw the arrival of the first double-deckers, two Leyland PD1s, and in 1951 the first underfloor-engine buses arrived. In 1960 the company purchased Ireland's first Leyland Atlantean, which was to be its last new bus purchase until 1971. The company began sourcing buses from UK operators, and initially these were Leyland Tiger Cubs and Leyland Royal Tigers. In 1968 the first Leyland Leopards arrived, and a total of 266 would enter service until 2001.

Above: **During 1953 Lough Swilly took delivery of four SARO-bodied centre-entrance Leyland PSU1/9s, Nos 75 to 78. This is No 77 (UI 5325) at Carndonagh Community School. It was rebuilt as a forward-entrance bus during 1969 and, after an exceptionally long service life, was withdrawn in March 1981.**

The next two new buses were the only Bristol LHs purchased. Second-hand purchases continued from CIE, Ulsterbus, Ribble and Trent. The last Leyland Atlantean, purchased from Oldham, arrived in 1980, but this was short-lived due to union opposition to one-person operation of double-deckers.

LOUGH SWILLY

Right: **On 1 June 1960 the first ever 30-foot double-decker supplied to any of the Wallace Arnold subsidiaries arrived at Kippax & District. It was a Leyland PD3/1, bodied by Roe and registered 6237 UB. On 31 March 1968 Kippax & District was sold to Leeds Corporation, which did not operate any of its buses. Lough Swilly acquired 6237 UB in 1968 and the bus was given fleet number 68; it is also seen at Carndonagh Community School. No 68 would have the distinction of being the last crew-operated bus in the Lough Swilly fleet, and was withdrawn from service in April 1982.**

Opposite: **In late 1976 Lough Swilly took on loan Ulsterbus No 382 (UZ 7382). This bus, a Leyland PSUC1/5T, was originally new to the Ulster Transport Authority in May 1957, with bodywork by UTA. It was purchased in September 1977, and is seen at Carndonagh Community School.**

Above: **In November 1977 Lough Swilly acquired from Ulsterbus 7425 UZ, a UTA-bodied Leyland PSUC1/12, new in March 1962.** It was given the fleet number 169 and is seen working the 16.20 journey from Letterkenny to Fanad Head, running along the eastern shore of Mulroy Bay, a lengthy sea loch and one of the most winding marine inlets in Ireland. The loch is well known for its fish and shellfish, in particular mussels, scallops and salmon. This section of route north of Kerrykeel is no longer served by any of Lough Swilly's scheduled bus operations.

Right: **This is No 140 (NZE 585), a CIE-bodied Leyland L2 that was new to CIE in October 1964 and purchased by Lough Swilly in November 1973. This view was taken at Derrybeg, with the bus operating the 13.50 journey between Letterkenny and Dungloe.**

Below: **Between 1977 and 1980 a small group of Duple Northern Bedford VAM 14s were acquired from Ulsterbus. Representative of these is No 181 (1254 TZ),**

which was new to Ulsterbus in May 1967 and acquired by Lough Swilly in July 1979. This view was taken at The Mosses, with No 181 operating the service between Letterkenny and Dungloe.

Right: **During 1979 the company purchased its penultimate Leyland Atlantean, an MCCW-bodied Leyland PDR1/1 new to Liverpool Corporation in December 1965 as its L737 (CKF 737C). This bus was given fleet number 177 and re-registered BUI 1497. No 177 is seen at Lough Swilly's Londonderry premises at Pennyburn, which was later vacated and redeveloped as a retail complex.**

Northern Ireland Road Transport Board/ Ulster Transport Authority/ Ulsterbus

The Northern Ireland Road Transport Board came into being on 1 October 1935, and was an early pioneer in the field of public ownership of transport. It was set up by the Government of Northern Ireland with a monopoly over all road transport in the province outside Belfast. Unlike London Transport, the NIRTB also had a road freight monopoly. By the end of the 1930s it had completed the takeover of all eligible bus and lorry operators.

In October 1948 the NIRTB and its fleet of around 900 buses, together with the entire rail network in Ulster, became the Ulster Transport Authority. Again, the buses, trams and trolleybuses of Belfast were not affected by this merger.

In April 1967 Ulsterbus Limited took over the bus and coach services of the Ulster Transport Authority. The fleet inherited was mixed, including significant numbers of half-cab buses, the last of which were not withdrawn until 1972. The oldest buses dated back to 1946 and the newest had entered service in 1965.

By 1939 the NIRTB had begun building its own bus bodies at its workshops at Duncrue Street in Belfast. Large numbers of Leyland PS1s with NIRTB bodywork were delivered new in 1947, an example being No A516 (GZ 6107), seen in Belfast in the livery of the Ulster Transport Authority in September 1963. No A516 would pass to Ulsterbus as No 516 in April 1967 and would remain with that company until early 1972. The bus next in line is No M607 (WZ 607), which was rebuilt by UTA in 1958 from the chassis of Leyland PS2/1 No C8894 (MZ 1965) to become a Leyland PD2/10c. A total of 158 Leyland PS2s were stripped of their bodywork and rebuilt as Leyland Titans using Metro-Cammell framed highbridge bodies, which were completed by UTA. No M607 was withdrawn from service in November 1971.

Right: The final bus bodied by the NIRTB was Leyland PS1 No B8729, in 1948. A total of 13 UTA-bodied Leyland PD2/10s, numbered E934 to E946 (OZ 2121 to 2133), entered service between July and November 1951, and seen in September 1963 is the last of the batch, No E946, which was withdrawn from service in 1967. The bus alongside is No A526 (GZ 6117), an NIRTB-bodied Leyland PS1 of 1947. Most of these half-cab single-deck buses were being, or had been, scrapped by the newly formed Ulsterbus, created in April 1967, as it modernised the fleet and bought new vehicles. However, GZ 6117 was one of several half-cab Leyland single-deckers that moved in 1967 from Ulsterbus to CIE. This was a most unusual sale, as CIE had never before imported any second-hand buses for its operations, but extra buses were urgently needed to enable the company to provide a new free school transport scheme being introduced by the Irish Government. A number of CIE's own half-cab single-deckers were also kept for the same reason. The Irish Government's longer-term plan was to fund the purchase of a dedicated fleet of school buses, mostly Bedfords, and the half-cab single-deckers were gradually withdrawn once the new Bedfords arrived.

Right: Between April and July 1953 37 UTA-bodied Leyland PSU1/11s were delivered. Leaving the seaside resort of Newcastle along Central Promenade on the run south to Kilkeel in September 1963 is one of this batch, No G8972 (OZ 845). The dog at the entrance to Annesley Court seems unconcerned by traffic! The large red-brick building in the right background is the impressive Slieve Donard Hotel and Spa complex, named after the highest peak in the nearby Mourne Mountains and opened in 1898 as a 120-room hotel for the Belfast & County Down Railway, which actively sought to entice passengers by also helping in the formation of the renowned Royal County Down Golf Club on adjacent links.

Above: A total of 119 Leyland Tiger Cubs were bodied by the UTA at Duncrue Works in 1956 and 1957. An example is No K348 (UZ 348), which entered service during 1957 and was later noted as being a driver training bus until its withdrawal in 1978. The next bus in line is No K714 (UZ 714), another of the Leyland PS2/1 rebuilds.

Below: This is No L405 (UZ 7405), a UTA-bodied Leyland PSUC1/5T that was new in 1957. This view, taken in September 1963, shows the Ulster Transport Authority depot in Greencastle Street, Kilkeel, County Down, with UZ 7405 about to be reversed alongside the office into the parking area behind the building. The depot is still in use, although the building no longer boasts the fine clock. The car on the right is a Vauxhall Cresta PA, more than 81,000 of which were built between 1957 and 1962. It was well equipped with leather and nylon upholstery for its bench front and rear seats, and woven pile carpet. A heater was fitted as standard, but the radio remained an option on the home market. Other options included fog lamps, reversing light, locking filler cap and external mirrors. In order to keep the front floor clear and seat six people in total, the handbrake lever was mounted under the dashboard and the gear lever was column-mounted. The car could be ordered painted in either single or two-tone colours, and cost £1,073 in 1958.

126 BUSES, TRAMS AND TROLLEYBUSES OF SCOTLAND & IRELAND

Right: **This view of UTA-bodied Ulsterbus Leyland PSUC1/5T UZ 7416, dating from 1957, was taken in Belfast in June 1975. This bus was destroyed at Ballycastle in December 1978.**

Below: **From 1967, for many years, the Leyland Leopard was the preferred choice of new single-decker for Ulsterbus, the vast majority being bodied by Potters or Alexander. Working on a Belfast Citybus route, and displaying Citybus logos, is No 1306 (4006 WZ), a Potter-bodied Leyland PSU3A/4R new in February 1969. In the background is the 113-foot-tall sandstone Albert Memorial Clock Tower, built between 1865 and 1869 by Fitzpatrick Brothers to a design by William Joseph Barre, an Irish architect who won a competition to choose a tower that would commemorate Queen Victoria's deceased consort Prince Albert. It was built on wooden piles on marshy reclaimed land, causing it to lean; in 2002 a multi-million-pound restoration project was completed, strengthening the foundations, replacing many of the carvings, and cleaning the entire tower.**

NIRTB/ULSTER TRANSPORT AUTHORITY/ ULSTERBUS

Above: During 1969 Potters was bought out by Walter Alexander Coachbuilders, and a subsidiary was set up called Walter Alexander & Co (Belfast) Ltd. The first single-deck buses to be built by the new company were a batch of Leyland PSU3A/4Rs, Nos 1341 to 1350 (AOI 1341 to 1350), delivered between September and December 1969. This view of No 1348 (AOI 1348) was taken in June 1975.

Below: Ulsterbus changed direction with its bus purchasing policy during 1973 and 1974 and purchased 200 lightweight buses, the order evenly split between the Bristol LH and the Bedford YRQ. All the buses, apart from two coach-bodied by Duple, received Alexander (Belfast) bus bodywork. This is No 1604 (FOI 1604), a Bristol LH6L that was new in July 1973 and is seen in Oxford Street, Belfast. The buildings on the left are part of St George's Market, and those on the right have since been demolished, to be replaced by part of the new Waterfront development.

Above: A large number of Alexander (Belfast)-bodied Leyland PSU3B/4Rs were delivered during 1972, and this is No 1574 (DOI 1574), seen in Londonderry during the early summer of 1979. This bus would be destroyed at Dungiven on 26 July 1982.

Below: In April 1979 Ulsterbus purchased four Metro-Cammell-bodied Leyland PDR1/1s from British Airways, which had been new to BOAC in 1966. They were numbered 951 to 954 in the Ulsterbus fleet and retained their registration numbers (LYF 306D, LYF 312D, LYF 315D and LYF 318D). Before entering service the large downstairs luggage compartment was removed and seating capacity was changed to 69. Seen in Londonderry shortly after entering service is No 953 (LYF 315D). This bus was later used as a driver trainer before being withdrawn in October 1985.